12-22-76

Moving towards *change*

Moving
towards *change*

*Some thoughts on the new
international economic order*

Unesco   Paris 1976

Published by the United Nations Educational,
Scientific and Cultural Organization
7 Place de Fontenoy, 75700 Paris
Printed by Imprimerie des Presses Universitaires
de France, Vendôme

ISBN 92–3–101365–3
*Le Monde en Devenir: Réflexions sur le Nouvel
Ordre Économique International* ISBN 92–3–201365–7
*El Mundo en Devenir: Reflexiones sobre el Nuevo
Orden Económico Internacional* ISBN 92–3–301365–0

Contents

1953284

Foreword

As Unesco completes the thirtieth year of its existence, the mission falling to it in the unstable world in which we live appears quite as important as it was when the Organization was founded just after the Second World War, if not more so. Unesco's essential function is still ethical, since its prime purpose is 'to contribute to peace and security by promoting collaboration among the nations through education, science and culture in order to further universal respect for justice, for the rule of law and for the human rights and fundamental freedoms which are affirmed for the peoples of the world, without distinction of race, sex, language or religion, by the Charter of the United Nations'.

Every passing day, however, shows up the dangers threatening peace. Expansionist trends persist in a variety of forms. Not only are tensions of all kinds—due to aggressiveness, violence, oppression and discriminatory practices—appearing or becoming more marked, but even armed conflict itself has not disappeared, and rages almost always in the most seriously disadvantaged areas. The arms race, swallowing up enormous sums of money which would be enough in themselves to enable us to do away with poverty and restore dignity to hundreds of millions of people, clearly runs directly counter to the efforts made to establish world peace on a basis of justice, equality and mutual respect. What is more, most of the resources allocated to scientific research are still directed to serving military ends. And in point of fact, this applies to both financial and human resources, since this death-centred research employs more scientists than any sector of production.

There are other threats, too, hanging over the world, deriving sometimes from the very powers that science and technology have conferred on man. Natural resources are very often exploited in a haphazard way, the background to life is deteriorating and the processes of extermination are being constantly perfected, achieving an unimaginable destructive power. Again, waste is tending to become the rule in privileged societies, whilst many peoples are sunk in stark destitution. Not a day passes but men, women and children die of hunger. Multitudes fall prey to diseases that modern medicine could perfectly well cure or even eradicate completely. It is therefore no exaggeration to say that the inequalities existing between countries or groups of countries, and within many countries too, are becoming intolerable. Furthermore, misunderstandings between cultures persist and in some instances are growing worse despite, or perhaps even because of, the gathering stream of information which sometimes seems likely to submerge us.

I am therefore convinced that, if these threats are to be averted, there must be a concerted, world-wide effort to address attention to the problems of the general future of mankind and the civilizations man has created, with a view to taking concerted action, too, on a world-wide scale. Over the past few months, this effort, so far as Unesco is concerned, has been in two main directions.

First—as I told the General Conference on taking up office that I intended to do—I set up a 'Panel of Counsellors' consisting of eminent people from all the major regions of the world. The terms of reference of this panel, which met three times in the first half of 1975, were to hold the widest and frankest possible exchange of views on the major problems at present confronting the world, on the way they interact, and on how international co-operation to solve them could be arranged. The report drawn up by the Panel of Counsellors at the conclusion of its work is appended.

Secondly, the Unesco Secretariat has made an analysis of the various problems with which the world is faced following important decisions taken by the United Nations, and I have drawn on this in the present paper. It will be remembered that the Member States of the United Nations, meeting from 9 April to 2 May 1974 for the Sixth Special Session of the General Assembly, solemnly proclaimed their 'united determination to work urgently for *the establishment of a new international economic order* based on equity, sovereign equality, interdependence, common interest and co-operation among all States, irrespective of their economic and social systems which shall correct inequalities and redress existing injustices, make it possible to eliminate the widening gap between the developed and the developing countries and ensure steadily accelerating economic and social development and peace and justice for present and future generations'. The Declaration and the Programme of Action on the establishment of a new international economic order,[1] which the General Assembly adopted at the end of this Sixth Special Session, and the resolution on development and international economic co-operation, which it adopted at its Seventh Special Session,[2] reflect the grave anxieties felt by developing countries at the general trend apparent in international economic relations. These resolutions stress the need for a radical change, which alone can offer hope of a better future. They mark a turning-point in the history of international economic relations although they also take up again some of the thinking which went with the international development strategy (adopted for the Second

1. Resolutions 3201 and 3202 (S-VI).
2. Resolution 3362 (S-VII).

Development Decade). Similarly, they tie in with, and consolidate, the work which led up to the adoption, by the United Nations General Assembly on 12 December 1974, of the Charter of Economic Rights and Duties of States.[1]

Studies in preparation for the establishment of a new international economic order have been the subject of attention not only from the various Specialized Agencies of the United Nations, each of which has endeavoured to make its own special contribution, but also from many national and international bodies, both official and private, which are alive to the breadth and urgency of the matter and its immediate relevance, and anxious to make their views known. This growth of awareness at various levels is a significant and encouraging phenomenon, for there can be no doubt that the changes needed will require long and patient efforts by all concerned. Nevertheless, while the general concept of a 'new international economic order' is now stimulating efforts and holding out hopes for the future, an enormous amount of work remains to be done if we are to see more clearly what it implies, gauge the obstacles to be overcome, define the most effective practical steps to be taken and foresee their consequences and, above all, give the idea impetus for the future. There would in fact be serious danger in going no further than broad statements of principle and verbal declarations, without doing anything to set the processes of change in motion. Enormous disappointment would then be felt. There is no pre-established pattern for a new international economic order which simply has to be applied. It has to be discovered on the basis of the most legitimate aspirations of the world's peoples. It will be built up gradually if a united determination continues to sustain the first enthusiasm and overcomes the difficulties which will inevitably arise when agreement has to be reached on the practical means of putting the idea into effect.

As a Specialized Agency of the United Nations, Unesco

1. Resolution 3281 (XXIX).

was in duty bound to make its contribution to the world community in order to further thinking and activities designed to promote the establishment of a new international economic order and, at the same time, to play the part properly falling to it as an adviser on matters within its special purview. There can, in fact, be no question of a new and more equitable world order unless due heed is paid to the requirements of education, science and culture, and full advantage taken of the light they can throw on problems. The General Conference of Unesco, having regard to the resolutions of the General Assembly, had in any case recommended that I 'arrange for Unesco to take part in the effort of reflection which is to be made in the United Nations with a view to strengthening the role played by the United Nations agencies in international economic co-operation and action to promote development'.[1]

The study which constitutes the main part of this booklet is an initial contribution by Unesco to this joint effort. It is principally intended, therefore, to advance thinking within the United Nations system and, of course, within the States belonging to intergovernmental organizations.

Nevertheless, it seemed to me that, because of the kind of problems dealt with and the way in which they have been tackled, this study might be of interest to a wider readership than those for which it would normally have been intended. For this reason, I have thought it well to arrange for this booklet to be circulated on a wider scale, since I feel that, if the world is to set about dealing, democratically, with the problems on whose solution its future and its very survival depend, it is vital that as many people as possible should appreciate what those problems are. It is with this in mind that the reader is invited to peruse the pages which follow.

In expressing my warm and sincere thanks to all those who have given me their assistance in the preparation of this work, I should like, in conclusion, to express my hope that

---

1. 18C/Resolution 12.1.

the community of interests which actually already exists among men through force of circumstances may develop into an active fellowship which will make it possible for us all to work together for a world of justice, progress and peace with due regard for the differences which represent the wealth of the various cultures and for the free self-determination of all peoples.

AMADOU-MAHTAR M'BOW
Director-General
Paris, January 1976   of Unesco

I

Efforts to arrive at a new international economic order

Facts and aspirations which have produced the concept

The idea of establishing a new international economic order was prompted, first, by objective observation of the fact that serious and sometimes desperate situations were affecting a major portion of the world's population and could not be allowed to continue without endangering peace, and, secondly, by the aspiration after greater justice, equity and fellowship apparent among the peoples suffering from these situations. These observations and aspirations led to a growing awareness of the need for change.

Without going over again in detail the diagnosis of the present international situation which has already been made on several occasions, it may be well to refer to its principal features. Unless they are fresh in people's minds, the concept of a 'new international economic order' is in fact liable to remain theoretical and speculative, whereas it is a response to a real factual situation calling for urgent measures to deal with it.

The growing disparity between the incomes of different countries (developed and developing) resulting from the conditions in which material goods are produced and the present system of international trade, is paralleled within each nation by inequality of distribution among the various social categories and frequently, too, by a discrepancy between town and country. The demarcation line between poverty and wealth does not, therefore, separate only countries into two groups but is found again within individual countries and between geographical areas. This dividing line between poverty (which in extreme cases may even go as far as destitution and famine) and wealth (which may take the form of opulence, luxury and waste) is no doubt not absolutely immutable. Over the past twenty years, some developing countries have had considerable economic growth rates and a few have suddenly found themselves with quite appreciable financial resources (derived from oil and raw materials), while the less fortunate remainder—in fact the majority—have seen their already precarious situation grow even worse. The same phenomenon can be seen with regard to the developed countries, whose situations and prospects for the future vary widely.

It is none the less true that these disparities are becoming intolerable and call for a change in the direction of greater equity.

Generally speaking, the 'international economy' is in a state of crisis, the repercussions of which are felt with varying degrees of severity in different countries. The most seriously affected are those which have least. The most powerful countries, by reason both of their reserves and of their influence, are managing to palliate the effects of the situation more successfully. The economic recession in industry and trade, the rapid progress of inflation, price and currency instability, and employment difficulties, are the most obvious symptoms of this crisis, which creates an atmosphere of uncertainty. Since crisis spreads like an infectious disease, this uncertainty is aggravated by economic interdependence, except in very large countries; and the temptation to look inwards and to revert to national protectionism is reappearing, with a consequent danger that rich and poor will become still more isolated.

The difficulties of the present situation are thus bringing home to people the need for a profound change which will substitute a juster and more equitable new order for the disorder at present prevailing.

The international system seems incapable of explaining and mastering the recent course of economic events. This is no doubt because that system is ill-adapted to the global dimension of the problems, to the legitimate aspirations of the new States and to peoples' needs. The basic tenets of economics themselves need to be reviewed in the light of the new economic, social and political facts. Whilst the aspiration after collective economic security is becoming widespread, with some parties anxious to retain or even to add to what they have gained and others desirous of attaining a better standard of living, individual nations, and even more, the international community, are still by no means able to make reliable forecasts. The future is not under control and the rational approach to socio-economic matters, to which programming and planning were tending, is being defeated by the hazards of the situation and the complexity of the factors involved in change.

Since the future can thus be glimpsed only with a considerable margin of uncertainty, despite the efforts made to clarify things scientifically, we have clearly reached a point at which political agreement among all countries—and not decision by a handful of them—is essential in making choices which concern the whole world community; and this presupposes a change in international political structures.

The need for such a radical change is all the greater because the political context in which the present economic order was worked out after the Second World War has now substantially altered. With the successive stages of political decolonization, new nations have won their independence but still have to consolidate it in the economic, social and cultural spheres. The emergence of many States which intend to take their full share of international responsibilities represents an irreversible change, to which the older nations must grow accustomed, not merely recognizing it officially in law but altering their own patterns of behaviour accordingly. The establishment of a new international economic order must be viewed in this new context and implies a critical examination of present international power (both institutionalized and *de facto*) and its reorganization.

All the nations have to face up to these world-wide challenges, which put the future of mankind at stake, whether the problems arise from population growth, the dangers of a deterioration of the natural and human environment, the genetic manipulation that scientific progress may make possible or the data-processing revolution, with its impact on communication and freedoms; or whether they are problems of yet other kinds. Such phenomena are likely to lead to profound changes in civilizations and cultures, and we may rightly wonder what kind of new society they may eventually produce.

Whatever hopes or fears this line of development may engender, it must not be regarded as being beyond man's control. It is important, above all, that the international community should strive to solve the problems arising in a way which will be beneficial to mankind as a whole, while taking all due account of the specific features and cultural individuality of each country.

The need to place in context and to broaden the concept

All these facts and aspirations make it necessary to work out a new type of international relations leading to a better appreciation of what the phrase 'new international economic order' really means. In outlining the possible form of such relations, we have first to consider the meaning and significance of each term in the phrase 'international economic order'.

*Economic problems are the starting-point
but we must be able to look beyond
this aspect of human affairs*

Appreciation of the need for change has grown out of the observation of economic facts and aspirations; and there is nothing wrong about this. People wish first of all to be able to live, and to have a better life, deriving advantage from the goods produced by modern industry, distributed on a fairer basis. One of the responsibilities of the political authorities is to see that their countries attain an adequate level of economic development. The preponderance thus accorded to economic problem can be justified by their urgency. If a new international economic order is to be established, however, the traditional conception of trade must be broadened and, what is more, economics must not be the only field considered.

At the present time, trade is no longer merely a commercial matter (consisting in the exchange of produce, the procedures and prices for which need to be determined on a more equitable basis) nor even a financial one (circulation of capital and relative position of currencies), although both these areas are extremely important. It cannot be divorced from such matters as the geographical and sectoral distribution of production capacity, which is itself linked with the various types of development (agricultural and industrial); the structure of consumption systems and the priority to be allotted to the production of commodities; the transfer and adaptation of technologies and 'home-grown' development of technology; the movement of specialists and the location of the 'poles of attraction' for trained scientific and technical brains.

All these problems, whose importance must not be underestimated, are bound up with a wider conception of society and indeed with a choice of civilization just as much as with economic regulations as such.

Again, whether it takes place between individuals or

between nations, trade ought to transcend the actual interests involved and take on again its profound human significance. The objects exchanged represent, first and foremost, communication between people, a positive acknowledgement of various kinds of interdependence, not passively experienced but actively sought, and an occasion for the exercise of practical fellowship. If the 'new international economic order' merely sets up more suitable machinery for the equitable regulation of international trade, it will not represent a proper appreciation of the kind of change to be made. In reality, it is the basic significance of trade, inspired by a sense of reciprocity and fellowship, which needs to be restored. This conception of trade prevailed for a long time in the traditional units (ethnic group, village, etc.) with a simple economic system covering a limited geographical area. Today, we have to rediscover modern ways of expressing this conception in complex, specialized economies on an international scale. If it is reduced to the establishment of regulatory machinery or to the reconciliation of interests, the 'new international economic order' is liable to be no more than a temporary expedient not soundly based, as it should be, on a critical examination of society itself. It was for this reason that the General Conference of Unesco, in its 18C/Resolution 12.11, laid emphasis on the socio-cultural factors involved in development and spoke of the establishment of a new international economic and social order.

All branches of the social sciences are thus required to assist in bringing out more clearly the factors and conditions which enter into the establishment of a 'new international economic order'.

The new order we are trying to establish also has a political aspect. In 18C/Resolution 12.11, the General Conference declared 'that the establishment of a new international economic order depends not only on political and economic factors, but also on socio-cultural factors, the role of which in development is constantly growing and which are crucial in the struggle of peoples against all forms of domination'.

The very purpose of a 'new international economic order' thus goes beyond the economic sphere proper; it is directed not only to making the best use of things and sharing them out more fairly, but to developing all men and women, and every aspect of the individual, in a comprehensive cultural process, deeply permeated with values, and embracing the national environment, social relationships, education and welfare. It is also concerned with providing a basis for the development of the international community itself.

Any effort to arrive at a new international economic order thus implies critical thinking about development, the significance and direction of which might well, no doubt, be redefined. The very fact that resources, whether or not renewable, are limited, shows, indeed, that the '"Western model of development" is not generally applicable either in space or in time. Progress based on this model, until now considered in certain quarters as being potentially capable of extension all over the world, is henceforth faced with fundamental contradictions.... We should look beyond economic development . . . [and] . . . give up thinking of the centres of economic power as the sole repositories of truth, civilization and universality' (Report of the Panel of Counsellors on Major World Problems and Unesco's Contribution to Solving Them).

The process of reflection involved in the establishment of a new international economic order goes still further, leading on to a critical examination of the growth model of industrial societies themselves. Such an examination is seen to be necessary by the highly industrialized countries, which have reached the stage of wondering whether it is possible to continue their expansion at the present pace, having regard to their consumption structures and their system of values. It also seems to be essential from the point of view of the developing countries, which, before starting on an intensive industrialization drive, are anxious to assess the cultural, social and human risks of such a venture.

The dynamism of the highly industrialized societies is in

fact based on a number of attitudes and beliefs which have hitherto been regarded as obvious and positive but are now beginning to be questioned, at least to some extent. The driving force of industrial societies is typified by a purely utilitarian kind of reasoning, based on the efficient application of scientific knowledge; by the conviction that there is no limit to man's ability to master nature and control the future course of societies' development by means of science and technology; and by a system of explanation which, in accounting for the state of the world, gives pride of place to the material forces of the productive system and subjects the whole of society to the demands of economic life, concentrating the power of decision in a few specially favoured centres.

The effort to arrive at a new international economic order thus leads on from economic premises to a searching consideration of the way in which it is desirable that societies should evolve, and of the principles and criteria which should govern our choices and actions. To this task, which rightly falls to the social sciences and philosophy, Unesco means to make a special contribution of its own.

An international or a world-wide scale?

In proclaiming their determination to establish a new international economic order, the United Nations have adopted a decision intended to lay down 'one of the most important bases of economic relations between all peoples and all nations' (Resolution 3201 (S-VI, para. 7)).

Despite this breadth of vision, the Declaration and Programme of Action are limited, since neither of them concerns the whole of economic life but only that part of the economy which involves international relations. The importance of this part, however, varies from country to country.

Although no nation can be entirely self-sufficient, the relative importance of international economic relations varies a great deal from country to country. Some great nations have relatively little external trade in comparison with their gross national product and are, for that very reason, less subject to the hazards of the international scene. They are, in addition, practically independent with regard to technology, finance, etc. The economy of other countries is more definitely oriented towards the outside world, mainly because of their inadequate industrial resources and the narrowness of their national markets, but also because of historical circumstances associated with colonization. International relations are, in such cases, preponderant.

As no nation can dissociate its external from its internal economic activity, and as every country has the right 'to adopt the economic and social system that it deems to be the most appropriate for its own development' (Resolution 3201, para. 4d) it may be well to consider the following question: On what bases are economic relations to be balanced between nations which have adopted differing or even opposing economic and social systems and which are asserting their independence as a means of promoting endogenous development?

The United Nations is no doubt called upon to establish a link between the two levels, national and international, but we cannot shut our eyes to the fact that a major difficulty is involved, inherent in the present conception of the community of nations and its organization. If this difficulty is to be overcome, three fundamental requirements must be taken into account.

First of all, the problems must be considered in a global context. As the Panel of Counsellors on Major World Problems and Unesco's Contribution to Solving Them stressed in its report: 'A global view must . . . be a prerequisite to any attempt to solve the different problems of today. . . . The world must be considered as a totality or a system, whose parts are organically linked. It is essential to consider the whole network of problems, in its interrelatedness and inner structure. . . . The first task of Unesco should be to stress the global character of these problems. It is not merely a question of promoting the idea of world-wide human solidarity as an ethical goal, but also, and above all, of furnishing an over-all interpretation of the world's problems, elucidating in particular the global nature of development.'

Second, an attempt must be made to identify the major world problems which exist or which are likely to arise, and to outline priority courses of action. If this is done, it will be possible to avoid making choices by reference to immediate problems alone and thus establishing a new international economic order which will prove unable to meet the challenges of the year 2000, for example, in many fields such as population, environment, education, the spread of scientific culture, employment, and the use of the oceans. It is important to bring to the fore an idea which has been gradually taking shape: that there is a heritage common to all mankind which we must find a way of administering together for the advantage of all. Until the consciousness of a transnational reality is more fully developed, there will be a temptation to rest content with compromise agreements between nations.

Third, national problems should be viewed in a more general context, and an order of urgency for their solution should be decided on in common. There is no doubt that the reduction of the economic inequalities among countries and within each one of them is a priority on which there should be general agreement.

The active agents in the work of reorganizing the world community are the nations, but at the same time new phenomena are making their appearance which seem in some respects to present a challenge to the present relations between nation-States. The most striking of these phenomena (but not the only one) is the development of large corporations with ramifications in many countries. The establishment of a new international economic order tends to involve regulating their operations under a code of conduct so as to control their activities and restrict the powers in the hands of private interests. Nevertheless, is not the emergence of such corporations an indication that, in one way or another, more and more activities will have to be considered against a background extending beyond the bounds of a single country, and will require to be managed in common for all nations?

The assertion of each nation's sovereignty over its natural resources and economic activities has to be reconciled—not in principle but in practice—with the recognition of growing interdependence. Sovereignty and interdependence cannot be conceived as complementary and mutually enriching notions unless a consciousness of world-wide solidarity develops, which should come closer to the expression of a common desire to live than to a peremptory demand for the righting of injustices or a fairer distribution of space, natural resources and goods.

At the present time, mankind is divided into an affluent minority in whom knowledge and power are vested, and the multitude of peoples aspiring after change; it is prey to many military conflicts, localized but presenting dangers for everyone. It tends to solve all problems by trial of strength; and does not yet clearly distinguish the threats hanging over the future. In such circumstances, the consciousness of the world's solidarity, which is so much needed, can only be the fruit of an active and continuous process of education, which must be put in hand without delay and to which Unesco must make its full contribution.

The need to elucidate the concept of 'order'

In the now set expression 'new international economic order', the word 'order' is the one most liable to lead to confusion. It is undoubtedly contrasted with the idea of 'old order', or even of 'present disorder'. It is important, however, to know on what basis the nations are agreed, since the word 'order' may have three quite different meanings, depending on whether it is taken as a type of organization, a legal structure, or a system of values.

In what sense is it taken in the official documents? In what sense should it be understood?

If we consider only the first meaning—the type of organization of international economic relations—the essential point is readjustment or modification of the present machinery. This modification may be brought about through a major change in relative strengths which is at present to be observed: the nations which have freed themselves from the colonial yoke quite rightly wish to transform the established order which operates to their detriment. But a change of this kind, if it were only a question of relative strengths, would scarcely have much stability. Although might has been right, for a long time, in the history of international relations, we seem now to have reached a point when, for the good of all mankind and even simply for its survival, we must, by agreement, move beyond that situation, in which violence is always ready to flare up.

It is tempting to base the new organization on an effort to find nations' common interests, to establish processes of dialogue and negotiation which will lead to practical agreements and the setting up of institutions. This is a practical, empirical method of procedure which does not necessitate knowing whether there is ultimate agreement on the substance of things, since it principally reflects the desire to solve practical problems. Nevertheless it would be illusory to suppose that nations easily reach agreement in recognizing common interests. It may probably be said that, in the long run, the interests of nations converge, but for immediate purposes they are more often at variance than they coincide. While they may overlap in a few fields where negotiation leads to compromise solutions, those solutions, though of no means negligible, remain precarious. Is it then possible to speak of an 'order', if it is based primarily on compromises? An 'order' of this kind will lack stability and permanence just because it is not more deeply rooted; and the agreements in which it is reflected are all too likely to be challenged as circumstances change.

The concept of 'order', in its second meaning, implies the idea of institutionalization based on the recognition of rights and duties. The legal order thus aims to give a society a more stable foundation, providing protection for everyone from the hazards of circumstance and from arbitrary action by authority. When we refer to the ideas of equality and democracy, and seek to reach agreement on 'codes of conduct' to regulate certain international activities, we are moving towards the establishment of an international legal order adapted to present trends. The proclamation, in December 1974, of the Charter of Economic Rights and Duties of States fits into this line of thinking, even though it is limited by the fact that there is no world authority able to see that these rights are applied, or even to enforce observance of them.

We must also give thought to a closer definition of the classic conception of 'rights', which often depends upon a particular philosophical view of man and society. The concept of equality of rights of which we hear so much is made meaningless by the countless inequalities in fact which are to be observed everywhere. A concern for true equality should give priority to promoting the rights of the most seriously deprived, and this must start by establishing equality of opportunity. The United Nations has no doubt been genuinely aware for some years past that some countries are much more seriously deprived than others, and special provisions have been made in official documents in an attempt to correct this imbalance; but this has most often been done from humanitarian considerations rather than in recognition of an actual right, that of the poorest to share in the world's wealth.

If a new international order is really to be established, there must first of all be agreement on a system of values and a willingness to embark on a joint examination of their implications: values of justice, equality, freedom and fellowship. These will be based on a new awareness in two respects, namely: recognition of the unity of mankind, with all its diverse peoples, races and cultures; and the assertion of a desire to live together, actually experienced not simply as a necessity for survival or coexistence but as the deliberate choice of fashioning a common destiny together, with joint responsibility for the future of the human race.

In the world of many cultures and ideologies in which we live, are the nations ready to agree on a 'system of values' which could be the foundation of a new order? This is a basic question, since only ethical considerations can induce States to leave behind the selfish pursuit of their own interests, which is so often a source of conflict, and the sometimes violent clashes arising from the assertion of power. Agreement on values is not easily reached: the use of the same terms may have behind it widely differing meanings and commitments. It is therefore in the interest of nations to listen to one another and to seek to understand each other, so that they may draw closer in these essential areas.

As changes come about very fast in political and social relations, and as there is constant progress in science and technology, an order based on legal provisions or on organization alone will soon cease to be suitable after a certain time—say ten years—and will therefore have to be continually reviewed. But if the system of values is taken as the basis, this new order will have a certain permanency although various phases of adaptation will be needed. Even if relative strengths change and if national interests find expression in different forms, not everything will then have to be reconsidered. Although they do not claim to be establishing an international order once for all, the various nations are seeking to set up a system of relations in which the continuity secured by the observance of enduring and universally recognized values will be inherent.

The Panel of Counsellors on Major World Problems rightly points out that: 'Of all the United Nations Specialized Agencies, Unesco has the most wide-ranging vocation; it is the only one in a position to consider contemporary problems in their world-wide context and in the light of their interdependence.' Unesco, being responsible for everything concerning knowledge, ideas and values, has, within the United Nations, the necessary authority to bring out the true dimensions of the effort to arrive at a new international economic order by linking together the three levels, namely: organization, institutions and law, and the system of values. '[As] Unesco's primordial concern should be the promotion of social justice . . . [it] must . . . use its best endeavours to ensure that the New International Economic Order is also translated into a New International Social or Human Order. . . . The ideas of responsibility, obligation, and duty, which are inseparable from the idea of rights, may lead to the conclusion that it is particularly important not only to set certain minimum standards, but also and above all certain maxima (e.g. in terms of consumption or income). The study of these limits is related to that of inequalities between nations and individuals and Unesco should promote such studies in preparation for the establishment of a world order based on justice.

Beyond the present studies with a view to the establishment of a new international economic order, something more serious is in the long run at stake. The survival of the world community is in the balance and, even while taking emergency measures to avoid a tragic outcome, 'is it not high time to display a certain modesty, a wisdom which at times our ancestors possessed and which could constitute the basis of a new morality? . . . To trigger off a moral awareness of these, especially in those highly industrialized countries whose excessive consumption of "resources" is speeding the destruction throughout the whole world of everything that represents life . . . we must try to go beyond short-term utilitarian solutions and conceive a fraternity based on an enduring sense of world-wide solidarity' (Report of the Panel of Counsellors on Major World Problems).

II

Obstacles and lines of action

The General Conference of Unesco, in Resolution 12.11 on the establishment of a new international economic order, adopted at its eighteenth session, realistically stated that 'prompt identification of the obstacles hindering development is vital if research programmes are to be successful. Attention will have to be devoted not only to the difficulties that developing countries are at present encountering in their economic advance but also to the new obstacles which will arise as a result of economic progress itself. The United Nations system will have also to identify obstacles which, because of the number of countries encountering them, or because they affect the whole world, could be overcome by concerted action in science and technology. Owing to its general responsibilities in this field, and its experience, Unesco has furnished assistance to Member States for this purpose and can render outstanding services to the United Nations system in the new function which the Programme of Action requires to be organized.'

In addition to the obstacles relating to development there are those which stem from the nature of international co-operation. Identification of both categories—not that this can be exhaustive, since new difficulties will continue to arise—will make it possible to indicate the courses to be followed for the establishment of a new international economic order.

Obstacles

To lay too much stress on obstacles or, on the contrary, to minimize them, are two attitudes that are equally lacking in realism. The obstacles which hinder the establishment of a new international economic order are of various kinds. Without seeking to provide a complete list of them, we offer some examples below.

The scope and vagueness of the expression 'new international economic order' lead to different—even divergent—interpretations, and this is an initial obstacle. For some people, this concept represents a sort of challenging utopia, no doubt fitted to give rise to reflection but destined to remain at the stage of principles and slogans. For others, Resolutions 3201 and 3202 adopted by the United Nations General Assembly at its Sixth Special Session propose precise procedures, essential for the establishment of more equitable international relations and forming a coherent whole; these provisions afford a sufficiently clear design to allow reference to *the* new international economic order. For others again, what is envisaged is a process of seeking *a* new international economic order.

The Panel of Counsellors on Major World Problems clearly saw the difficulty, when it pointed out in its report that the expression 'new international economic order' at the present time 'covers different realities, interests and intentions: a classification is therefore desirable'. Hence the suggestion of initiating fundamental discussions—for which Unesco would have responsibility—on certain basic aspects of the 'new international economic order'. It is important not to give credence too readily to a consensus; it is, at times, purely verbal as is shown by the diversity of interpretations.

'By shying away from all subjects of disagreement we allow them to worsen of their own accord.'

A further difficulty of interpretation resides in assessment of the present situation and of the evolution that has taken place over the past thirty years. Here again there is latent divergency on several points.

In the eyes of some people, the present international situation seems to be so fraught with difficulties, disparities and uncertainties that it can only be characterized as disorder—disorder which must be replaced by a new order. Others, without denying the present difficulties, consider that in magnifying them we lose sight of the positive aspects of an evolution in the course of which some developing countries have made real advances in regard to standards of living, knowledge, health, etc. According to yet others, lastly, the question of whether a new economic order is necessary or whether it suffices to maintain the old one is a subject of fruitless discussion. It is better to look towards the future, to shape the present world and to seek a consensus on the realities and principles of the endeavour to achieve development.

Opinions differ also on the interpretation to be given to the history of recent decades. Some people have no hesitation in condemning the developed countries as a whole for their previous behaviour and in placing entire responsibility for the present situation on their shoulders, demanding, in particular, compensation and restitution in respect of a wrongful exploitation of natural resources and human potential. Others find it difficult to agree with so total a responsibility, which seems to them to lack sufficient historical justification, or any fair weighing up of the pros and cons. What would have happened, they say, if the developed countries had not intervened at all? While it is impossible to rewrite history on the basis of hypotheses, it is difficult to assess it fairly since every nation has lived through it in a different way. It is not a matter of two aspects of a single reality. The interpretation of history divides more than it unites.

There is divergence again in the analysis of the causes of the crisis. For some people, the main reason for it is the determination of the developed countries to maintain their privileged position, their power, their scientific and technical advance, even to the point of supporting this with a show of military might, whereas, in a context of co-operation aiming at a fairer distribution of wealth, opportunities and power, each nation must be able to take its own destiny in hand, relying firstly on its own resources, and to secure its own development in its own particular way. For others, it is uncontrolled population growth that slows down and jeopardizes economic progress and that gives rise to formidable employment and unemployment problems. Lastly, some people think that the crisis resides primarily in industrial society itself, at least in its present forms.

A further obstacle: the rigidity of economic structures. Since the end of the Second World War, efforts have been made to adapt these: international Specialized Agencies have been established to deal with the various aspects (commercial, industrial, monetary, etc.). Numerous conferences and meetings have been held, but they have not succeeded in overcoming the increasing complexity of the factors involved or in finding innovatory solutions to the problems. This gives rise to a feeling of defeat, frustration and revolt in regard to a system which it seems difficult—even impossible—to change radically enough to secure a greater equity.

The centres of power and decision-making are indeed many and varied, without being co-ordinated or coherent. Although States meet regularly in the Agencies of the United Nations system, other types of meetings, bilateral and multilateral, retain all their importance. Depending on the economic system chosen, private organizations have an autonomous existence and a capacity for action in their own right, which is at times considerable when these are, for example, transnational companies or international associations of scientists and technicians. Lastly, in more than one sector, international opinion, due to the efforts made in the sphere of communication and information, is beginning to have some weight.

If there is a real desire to prepare the way for a change-over to a new international economic order, these different vectors of action will have to be co-ordinated.

Among the phenomena that largely affect the possibility of establishing a new international economic order, particular mention should be made of the accumulation throughout the world of vast armaments resources and of the consequent trade in weapons of war. Related to the level of industrialization, this process comprises a complex system of production and exchange of power and hegemony. Since, moreover, the will to peace must necessarily accompany the establishment of a new international economic order, of which it is a determining factor and a fundamental aim, this dimension of the problem and the real obstacle that derives from it cannot be disregarded.

As the Panel of Counsellors on Major World Problems suggests in its report, 'Unesco should promote studies on ways of reconverting the armaments industry into peaceful activities, giving special attention to the manner in which this might be achieved under various social and economic systems, with minimal detriment to the workers and scientists now engaged in this industry. . . . Special concern should be given to the possibility of forbidding or at least reducing the arms trade.'

As much as in the rigidity of structures, the obstacle resides in attitudes of mind. These must be changed so as to develop an awareness of the immensity of what is at stake for the whole word. A very extensive endeavour will have to be launched, for the information of those people who are at the head of affairs and those who exert an influence on public opinion. Unesco has an important part to play in this connexion, in conjunction with States.

In particular, the persons in authority in the developed countries still seem little disposed to accept all the practical consequences of a new international economic order. Mindful as they are of the international tasks which they alone have been performing for so long, it is more difficult for them to think in terms of sharing—sharing of goods and knowledge, of course, but—above all—sharing of the power of decision as regards choice of objectives and means. What is comprised in a 'new international economic order' is, however, all these different areas of sharing and co-responsibility. We must therefore seek to intensify the change in attitude that is beginning to be apparent.

Another obstacle to be overcome: the present structures for working and for decision-making within the United Nations system. There is no chance of a new international economic order establishing itself spontaneously, by tacit agreement on the part of all parties and without an endeavour by the international agencies to promote it. To believe this would be utopian. How then, while safeguarding the sovereignty of each State and in the absence of a world political authority, can the United Nations system be strengthened and adapted so as to fit it for the promotion of a new international economic order?

The task is all the more difficult in that the United Nations system was set up, historically, on the initiative of the developed countries and therefore to a large extent in accordance with their international strategies (commercial, technological, financial, etc.), leading to the gradual integration of other economies into a system administered and dominated by the industrialized countries. This standpoint, which explains the present structures of the United Nations system, is further reflected in the International Development Strategy (1970), based on the assumption that the development of the Third World would be obtained through integration in the world economic system. This assumption has been disproved by events. The projected integration has increased dependence and reduced the autonomy of the developing countries inasmuch as it has induced them to produce what 'the international system' wanted them to, rather than what they themselves needed. Development of this kind through integration and the servile copying of different kinds of needs is rejected today, and what is sought, on the contrary, is the strengthening of the capacity for development inherent in the Third World. This Copernican revolution reveals the contradiction that exists between the underlying dynamics of the international system, revolving round the developed countries, and the real requirements of the developing countries. Hence the need for a revision of the structures (and the spirit) of the United Nations system.

These major issues were the subject of initial reflection by the United Nations General Assembly at its Seventh Special Session, and the various Specialized Agencies of the United Nations were invited to give their views (see chapter III of this document dealing with 'the adaptation of the United Nations system').

Lines of action   1953284

If we are to establish a new international economic order, various lines of action must be opened up, for which the consensus of all the nations appears to be necessary.

Acceptance of a genuine commitment to a new form of international co-operation

The basis and purpose of the demand for a new international economic order is a redistribution of resources and power. Two courses can be contemplated: opposition between developed and developing countries, or genuine and constructive co-operation.

The first course is based on bargaining strength: those on the stronger side use their dominant position, temporary or permanent, to their own advantage. To take this line—to accept this state of affairs—would mean giving evidence of an inability to achieve changes based on equity and mutual respect. It would mean admitting a failure on the part of the United Nations, one of whose tasks it is to show countries how to co-ordinate their interests and to promote peace with justice and respect for all. Economic opposition can only lead to new inequalities, sufferings and the risk of serious conflicts, at a time when larger and more effective military potentials are available to back up or replace economic power.

Co-operation is seen to be the only reasonable line to take, once there is realization of the close interdependence of national economies, the limited nature of world resources, and the unprecedented dangers for mankind that would be entailed by new conflicts.

Between co-operation and opposition, some countries —or groups of countries—sufficiently able to stand alone might think of another course: that of withdrawal. A withdrawal leading to almost total isolation is hardly conceivable today. But a nationalist retirement behind frontiers and an endeavour to secure the greatest possible self-sufficiency in fundamental economic spheres (energy, raw materials, food resources, information system and even technological know-how) are real temptations at the present time: neither opposition nor co-operation but coexistence without too many clashes and with no external responsibilities, each one relying on its own sources of strength. This means carrying the notion of self-reliance to extremes and making it possible for the great powers to retire within themselves, while the needs of the poorer countries and the challenging situations that might arise in the world would be disregarded. This line appears to be neither morally acceptable nor, in the long run, realistic.

If opposition is to be avoided and co-operation facilitated, instruments must be created that are fitted to serve the purposes of joint consultation, negotiation and to some extent arbitration. Co-operation does not exclude the continued existence of states of tension, recognition that interests may differ or even clash, or discussion on priorities and means of action, even if agreement is reached on the ultimate objectives and phasing. But it does imply an enduring and practical determination to take the way of dialogue and conciliation.

Arrangements for setting up, on an international scale,
a structure able to promote the establishment
of a new international economic order

At the present time, international economic relations are based on power structures which tend to ensure, if not to strengthen, their continuity. What is needed is a new power structure, based on the will of each country to be master of its resources and sovereign in the choice of its economic and social system, on the rejection of any form of external domination and, at the same time, on the desire for co-operation with other countries and the assumption of responsibility towards challenging situations that may arise in the world.

The international community should provide itself with a power structure resting on democratic and representative foundations. A new international economic order cannot be established without the dynamic operation of an organized system representing the interests of the whole world and possessed of the necessary authority, legitimacy and resources.

There is a great difference between the ability of the respective nations to influence and to bring about changes in international economic relations. The setting up of equalizing instruments, in the economic sphere by means of regional or sectoral groupings, may help to avoid a worsening of the present disparities. If, however, these equalizing instruments are to further joint interests rather than sectoral interests, they must be established within the United Nations itself.

A strengthened power structure at international level would make it possible to draw up, with more chance of its being effective, a plan in which the efforts of the various Specialized Agencies would converge instead of being juxtaposed and sometimes in competition. Moreover, international economic relations would then be provided with instruments more closely akin to planning procedures than to market mechanisms. This is a necessity from the technical point of view (the problems to be solved call for an interdisciplinary approach), from the economic and social points of view (the oligarchical structure of the modern market serves the aims of capitalist enterprises, whether private or State, or, indirectly, the interests of the rich countries to the detriment of the most deprived peoples), and from the political point of view (the instruments of 'free exchange' favour the strongest, so that planning is essential to allow of participation by the weakest countries which are in the majority).

Integration of the changes to be made,
at international and at national level

There is an obvious and reciprocal link between the social and economic development of each country and its economic relations with other nations. Since, in addition, international economic activity represents only a part—larger or smaller as the case may be—of national economic activity, it would be illusory to seek to meet the legitimate aspirations of the respective peoples by proceeding to change only international economic structures. The result might well be limited and disappointing. Parallel with the trend favourable to the establishment of a new international economic order, and with each country's acceptance of it, it is necessary to create a current of thought which would be conducive to a change in the social and economic structures of each country so as to provide for a more equitable internal distribution of resources.

In certain cases, external aid and the reform of international economic relationships (commercial, financial, etc.) have only contributed, in the developing countries, towards strengthening the power and resources of a minority and have not benefited the population as a whole, which is mainly rural. It is for this reason that, with due regard for the sovereignty of every nation, it is necessary, for an assessment to be made within the United Nations, of the repercussions of international decisions on the evolution of national economies and on the internal distribution of resources.

A clearer definition of this integration and the adoption of appropriate measures would seem to be essential for the success of the new international economic order.

Promotion of co-operation between the developing countries

One of the principles contained in the Declaration on the Establishment of a New International Economic Order is: 'the strengthening, through individual and collective actions, of mutual economic, trade, financial and technical co-operation among the developing countries, mainly on a preferential basis' (Resolution 3201 (S-VI)). This line of action is specified in the Programme of Action (Resolution 3202 (S-VI)), where it is stressed that collective self-reliance and growing co-operation among the developing countries will strengthen their role in a new international economic order. It was also confirmed by the United Nations General Assembly at its Seventh Special Session: 'Developed countries and the United Nations are urged to provide, as and when requested, support and assistance to developing countries in strengthening and enlarging their mutual co-operation at sub-regional, regional and inter-regional levels' (Resolution 3362 (S-VII, Part VI, para. 1)).

For its part, the General Conference of Unesco, in Resolution 12.11 adopted at its eighteenth session, invited the Director-General: 'to study the developing countries' programmes for mutual co-operation and their experience in this respect, and to promote and foster such co-operation with a view to the establishment of a new economic order'.

All genuine progress towards a new international economic order requires the developing countries to improve and develop their own machinery with a view to taking part in negotiations with the developed countries. Responsibility for this lies in the first place with the developing countries. This co-operation between developing countries, through horizontal relations, can extend to many sectors: co-ordination of industrial and agricultural development policies and intensification of trade, strengthening of a capability for financial independence, gradual establishment of a joint monetary system, improvement of technical capabilities by means of innovation, creation and the adaptation and use of knowledge, strengthening of autonomous communication channels, etc.

Special concern for the needs of the poorer countries

For some years past, the United Nations has made a point, at its different meetings, of taking regularly into consideration the situation of the least advanced countries. A typology of marginality in under-development has been worked out: least-developed countries, land-locked and island countries, and countries most seriously affected by the crisis, for which special or urgent programmes must be put in hand.

This concern marks an advance in international awareness. Stress should be laid upon it, so that the inclusion of such words in texts may not be merely a stylistic addition but may have practical consequences. In global objectives, priority must be given to these nations, not out of pity inspired by crying poverty, but out of social justice and of a desire to lessen this marginality or at least to prevent it from worsening, until such time as those profound modifications have occurred which will change the situation for all countries and peoples that are suffering from the present inequalities. In this particular kind of active fellowship all the other countries should take part, and it should be one of the significant tests of the success of a new international economic order.

Instigation to participation by all

While it is the States that are essentially interested in the establishment of a new international economic order, and while it is through their representatives at the United Nations that discussions are held and commitments entered into, nothing can be easily put in hand if the consensus is not shared by the various (private or public) professional, cultural, social, political and even religious organizations, and if individuals themselves are not informed of the extent and originality of the proposed changes so that they can assess their advantages and their cost. Decisions emanating solely from an authority would have a limited effectiveness; the change must come about as a result of a general impulse.

This is why, in keeping with its purpose, Unesco should develop a suitable system of information and education in order to communicate messages to world public opinion concerning the establishment of a new international economic order. It is essential to persuade public opinion that 'problems are global, that the world in all its diversity is a universe of interdependent factors, that there exists a fundamental solidarity between human beings, and that solutions based on conciliation serve the interests of everyone'. (Report of the Panel of Counsellors on Major World Problems.)

Special mention should also be made of private international organizations, whether economic, social, cultural, scientific, or of any other kind. Through their very structure, these organizations are particularly fitted to understand international relations and—it may be hoped—the need for change. Provided that they resist both the temptation to intervene in the political life of nations and the temptation to seek to impose trends or choices which are in line with their own interests, it is desirable that they should feel themselves connected or even associated with the changes which will have to be made with a view to the establishment of a new international economic order and that, in the case of each of them, an awareness and a programme of activities will lead to convergence and not to dispersal of efforts. Unesco has a role to play in this respect.

From this point of view, it is impossible to overemphasize the importance of the long-established collaboration between Unesco and the international non-governmental organizations. The close association of the latter with the Organization's activities has made it possible for Unesco to go beyond its intergovernmental framework by forging links with representative elements of the international intellectual community and of national communities which have brought it fresh aid while giving it the opportunity to extend its influence in return. It is important that this co-operation should continue to expand, since one cannot avoid noting that too many non-governmental organizations have national branches only in countries which meet too narrow a set of geopolitical criteria. A situation of this kind is unacceptable in the context of the establishment of a new international economic order; effective participation by the Third World countries in the life and activities of these organizations is clearly a major objective.

Provision for transitions

A radical and instantaneous change with a view to the immediate establishment of a new international economic order is not feasible. Owing to the complexity of situations, the interdependence of the various spheres and the absence of any world authority, a world-wide economic revolution is out of the question. Provision must therefore be made for stages and for transitions, with, however, the underlying prospect of change on a world scale.

If, for example, it is desired to effect a geographical redistribution of world industrial potential so that it is more equitably shared out among the various nations—as was advocated in the Lima Declaration adopted by the Second World Conference of the United Nations Industrial Development Organization (UNIDO) in March 1975—it will be necessary to choose a distant horizon (the year 2000) and to have recourse to a process of planned transition, so as to avoid the disadvantages of changes which are too sudden both for industrialized and for developing countries. For industrial redeployment to be a credible venture, its difficulties must be foreseen and attenuated.

The same applies to all the problems concerning education and the changing of attitudes. A sudden change is scarcely conceivable, and this is precisely why the successive stages must be determined and the successive activities realistically spaced out.

The transition to a new international economic order will imply negotiations and discussions between industrialized countries and developing countries. Time-tables, agendas and, above all, the means of implementation will have to be decided on, with a judicious co-ordination of short-term and long-term objectives. While it would be illusory to remain at the stage of principles or to plan vast and distant transformations, it is also important to avoid becoming completely absorbed by immediate problems and, in an attempt to solve them, adopting a host of partial or even heterogeneous solutions which, far from promoting the establishment of a new international economic order, would, by a dispersal of effort, blunt the intention to effect an over-all change.

III

Adaptation of the United Nations system

If the United Nations system wishes to contribute to the transformation of the world economic and political context and international relations so as to respond effectively to the aspirations expressed in the declaration and the guidelines set out in the Programme of Action (Resolutions 3201 and 3202 (S-VI)), it must acquire the necessary means and hence, to a certain extent, adapt to new situations.

Such adaptation is, in any case, in the order of things. Gradually, as new problems have arisen, various institutions, funds and specialized programmes have been added to the United Nations system, which was conceived immediately after the Second World War. The whole imposing, complex and unwieldy structure needs to be thought out afresh, a few major priority fields of action which correspond to its permanent purpose being taken as the focal point. It is not enough to alter details or to make changes as a concession to conflicting influences. If the United Nations wishes to strengthen its credibility in the eyes of States—especially new States—and in the eyes of the peoples and international public opinion, it must show that it is adaptable.

For the establishment of a new international economic order implies the transformation of international social and economic structures. Over and above declarations of principle (even if they are unanimous) the United Nations system, if it is to achieve practical results, as we all hope it will, must have a certain minimum of authority and also new political and economic machinery, so that, while respecting the sovereignty of States, it may take the necessary action and establish genuine international co-operation with a view to development. All nations must be called upon to participate on an equal footing in this task, which is the responsibility of the whole world community, and they must be aware of their specific responsibilities and take care to see that there is democratic representation within the various bodies.

If we are to set up a new international economic order, we must be ready to undertake a sincere and courageous reassessment of the whole of the United Nations system. Unesco proposes to contribute to this reassessment—which is now taking place, in accordance with the recommendations made by the group of experts appointed to study structural changes within the United Nations system (Resolution 3343 (XXIX)) by giving its support in three fields: the adaptation of structures and institutions so as to cope with the new tasks implicit in the establishment of a new international economic order; the elaboration of criteria for United Nations action and the examination of its means of action, and efforts to increase the financial resources available to the United Nations and improve the management of these resources.

The adaptation of structures and institutions

While acknowledging the importance of the study submitted by the group of experts and the value of several of its recommendations, one may regret that the establishment of a new international economic order was not in the forefront of its deliberations. For if we are content to remodel existing structures we shall never be able to endow the United Nations with a role and resources commensurate with the projected new economic order; nothing but genuine renewal will do.

The reform of structures and institutions should be based on three major principles: the establishment of a new international economic order must be adopted as a priority project; all Member States must be more effectively represented in the system's institutions, so as to strengthen their right to be heard; and co-ordination among these institutions must be improved, so that they will be more effective.

On the basis of these three principles a redefinition of criteria and means of action can be proposed and an increase of financial resources sought. These three principles, too, will inspire all Member States with fresh confidence in the United Nations system and the secretariats of its institutions and Agencies, to which they will give their unreserved support.

Because of the magnitude, complexity and urgency of the social and economic problems raised by the new international economic order, the United Nations system must take on three new roles in the service of the international community—those of forward planning, joint discussion and programming.

Forward planning

Today, the danger lies in letting our attention be taken up with immediate problems such as inflation and the production crisis, currency fluctuations, instability in the price of raw materials, difficulties in agriculture, etc. Their urgency of course calls for great attention, and rapid steps must be taken in the sectors concerned. But the serious medium- and long-term problems would be quickly forgotten, and no thought would be given today to the principles underlying solutions which, if left till tomorrow, will prove to be too late. A new international economic order cannot be built up on the events of the present situation, even if these are symptoms of more profound troubles. We must seek out the real causes and, above all, plan for a long time ahead. If we try to deal with the most pressing difficulties, we shall find ourselves with a series of empirical but disparate measures which will not fulfil the profound aspirations of States and of peoples. We shall have merely plastered over the cracks, whereas what we must do is to lay the foundations for a real strategy of change.

The United Nations system should gather together basic information as to how society's permanent problems are evolving, not only problems of economics but also those of science, education, communication, population, health, working conditions and the distribution of income, the aim being to centralize the data collected, compare them and conduct interdisciplinary studies of them.

Going beyond these data, the volume of which would, in any case, quickly become a paralysing burden, surveys of the world situation and 'scenarios of the future' should be made, using various basic hypotheses. This task—the provision of information analysis and prediction—should be carried out in close contact with States and with the various centres for analysis and forward planning. It is more important to see the future clearly than to regulate the present and mitigate, as far as possible, the harmful effects of crises. Our view of the future will always have a considerable element of uncertainty in it, but the aim of forward planning is precisely to reduce this uncertainty, though it cannot be eliminated. If people today are to act, and not become anxious or rebellious, they need some degree of assurance about the future. If the future is wrapped in darkness, it engenders uncontrolled fear, and fear gives rise either to violence or to submission to authoritarianism in its various forms.

It is the responsibility of the United Nations system to

help shed light on the future, since today all nations and all peoples, by reason of their interdependence, share a common future.

Joint discussion

The United Nations system has given proof of its ability to inaugurate dialogue between Member States so that the broad lines of action of the international community can be seen. It should also provide an excellent context for bilateral or multilateral meetings, and for joint discussion of specific problems, which would thus be seen in relation to general objectives. Of course, joint discussions already take place on certain clearly defined problems (essentially economic problems), but their range must be widened considerably. There could, for example, be discussions of this kind on matters of science, technology, education, communication and the environment. Although communications are so highly developed, it is still true that people are cut off from each other, and unless someone takes the initiative in arranging meetings and discussions individuals and nations may remain enclosed within their own ideas and their own plans. Facilities for international discussions must be developed and there must be more places for them to be held. It would certainly also be a good thing if we combined our efforts to tackle certain fundamental problems concerning mankind's economic, genetic, scientific, cultural and moral heritage, so as to move towards a consensus on the major issues of our time.

Programming

It is vital for the institutions of the United Nations system to continue their attempt to bring the medium-term programming of their activities into line, since this will make it possible to reach the desired aims more effectively. It would also be advisable to prepare certain sectoral programmes for the system as a whole.

With the International Development Strategy, the General Assembly and the Economic and Social Council of the United Nations demonstrated the value and the feasibility of planning long-term strategies. Using these over-all views as a starting-point, real programmes with successive objectives should be prepared, and they in turn should be co-ordinated to form sectoral programmes which the Specialized Agencies would have to work out in detail and put into practice.

Programming of this kind, in which the national programming of the countries themselves would of course be taken into account, would make it possible to see the true priorities more clearly and to adapt the allocation of financial and human resources, more successfully. Such programming would also help the various countries to work out their own objectives, taking account of what is planned at the international level.

Detailed and flexible co-ordination between programmes and resources will be needed, so that resources can be employed as effectively as possible. A programme without sufficient resources is immediately impaired; but resources sometimes become available without detailed programmes having been planned, and in that case the resources are not effectively used.

In order to perform these new functions more efficiently, the United Nations system should make the machinery at its disposal more effective, while taking care to avoid the dangers of bureaucratization, excessive centralization and loss of contact with reality which threaten any large organization.

In taking action which is the responsibility of the United Nations system, therefore, the following principles should be observed:

Care should be taken to ensure that action to modify international economic and financial relations (International Monetary Fund, United Nations Conference on Trade and Development, General Agreement on Tariffs and

Trade) and the financial assistance given to the various sectors of national economies are complementary.

The decision-making structures of the various bodies concerned should work together, and steps should be taken to secure the participation of all countries in making these decisions. The present disparities in the system whereby developing countries participate are a hindrance to the extension of efforts to the whole world.

The function—which the United Nations system should exercise—of eliciting international financial contributions to development should be developed. The World Bank and its branches should act in a specific way, differing from that of the major private investors, but in co-operation with them if necessary; they should not simply aim to make investment profitable, but should encourage it.

New definition of the criteria and means of action of the United Nations

The methods of 'assistance' used in the United Nations system date from the First Development Decade, and should be revised. They enable knowledge to be transferred from one country to another rather than stimulating the beneficiary countries' own potentialities. In particular, the idea of projects with traditional components (experts, equipment, fellowships) is not always the best suited to the needs of endogenous development, in view of the social and cultural implications of the contributions made. It would certainly be preferable to incorporate external contributions into national programmes in which the establishment and development of research, the training of personnel and the spread of progress would all play their part. In this way, external contributions would be better integrated with national development plans.

Apart from emergency aid (10 per cent of available

resources), the United Nations system above all provides pre-investment, leaving it to other sources to provide the investment proper. In practice, however, it is impossible to separate these two aspects. The question as to where the investment will come from must be asked as early as the pre-investment stage, in relation to national plans. In addition, the United Nations system should also be able to make provision for investment programmes (in whole or in part).

The executive capacity of the United Nations system should be increased, both qualitatively and quantitatively, so that it can satisfy directly requests made by developing countries, particularly for projects concerning the establishment of a new international economic order.

For this purpose, the system should be given the necessary means:

To set up an insurance system so as to guarantee contracts concluded by developing countries with firms in developed countries, wherever this type of action is preferred by the national authorities concerned.

To establish, in co-operation with governments, a programme of action relating to raw materials and energy, in order to stabilize the price of manufactured products sold to developing countries and to reorganize trade and international transport so that they are based on genuine equity.

To encourage the establishment of multinational institutes that will undertake research which it is not to the advantage of developed countries to carry out, raise the standard of technological knowledge and make it available to national users at lower cost.

To prepare and implement, as soon as possible, a staff training plan so that developing countries can see to their own development at the various stages of production.

To enable member countries to protect themselves from the harmful effects which may be attendant upon the activities of transnational corporations.

To support the economic growth of States which have
recently gained their independence.

To encourage the establishment of a new international monetary system, universal in nature, ensuring equitable
participation by the developing countries.

In order to contribute to a gradual and more balanced redistribution of world resources, the United Nations system
should have the necessary resources (studies and execution)
in the following fields:

Buffer stocks of a large number of basic products should be
built up, under international control, in accordance
with the recommendations made by the Secretariat
of the United Nations Conference on Trade and Development.

There should be a joint financing system, providing adequate
guarantees, for building up stocks.

There should be a system of medium-term multilateral
undertakings (which should include an accepted price-
range) for the purchase and sale of basic and industrial
products among producing and consuming countries.

There should be a competitive system of finance to take
account of the fact that not all products from all
countries would necessarily benefit from the above-
mentioned procedures.

There should be a system to protect developing countries
from the harmful consequences of inflation and currency
fluctuations.

Increasing the financial resources
which should be available
to the United Nations system

In order to carry out the tasks involved in the establishment
of a new international economic order, the United Nations
system should have much greater financial resources at its

disposal. These resources, which are small in relation to the bilateral financial flows noted by the Development Assistance Committee of the Organization for Economic Co-operation and Development (about one-fifth), are today insufficient and poorly used because of the great number of funds from which they are drawn.

Within the United Nations system, institutions such as the United Nations Capital Development Fund and (within the World Bank Group) the International Finance Corporation should stimulate flows of capital towards the developing countries. Neither of them as yet has more than very modest resources.

A considerable effort must be made to mobilize financial resources for developing countries. Bilateral negotiations between countries possessing resources and countries seeking capital (especially those most affected by the crisis) are to be encouraged. But the United Nations system should not merely play the part of a catalyst in this bilateral action. Its Specialized Agencies must be provided with adequate financial resources to implement programmes for the reorganization of the international economic system and the restoration of a proper balance between the various regions. Certain developing countries which now have more considerable resources are in any case already making an effective contribution to the intensification of this effort.

These increased resources would also make it possible to participate not only in the necessary adaptation of the economic structures of the developed countries which will come about as a result of the establishment of a new international economic order, but also in urgently needed innovations in developing countries (financing the buffer stocks of raw materials, for example).

However, the desire to establish a new international economic order also implies the establishment, within the United Nations framework, of a new fund having the necessary resources to make such a vast project successful. This must be associated with a policy for world-wide peace.

For it would be an illusion to dream of a new international economic order if the arms race were to continue, absorbing considerable capital for dangerous undertakings, and if the political conditions for world-wide peace were not actively sought, excluding any idea of hegemony or domination by one nation over another. The reduction of armaments would, on the contrary, enable sums of money to be freed which could be put towards the establishment of a new international economic order. The constitution of the fund whose establishment is suggested should be based on the change-over of war industries to a peace-time economy.

Other means of finance other than a fund of this kind could be considered. Some have been mentioned by different governments—for instance, the allocation of funds obtained from the exploitation of mineral resources from the ocean bed (soil and subsoil).

Furthermore, it is obvious that this fund should in no way, by the loans it would make, increase the external debt of the developing countries, which is already excessively burdensome. It should make long-term, low-interest loans available to firms in the countries which have contributed to its establishment, and should finance United Nations activities and programmes for developing countries.

The establishment of a United Nations Fund of this kind, having increased resources, administered under the direct control of the representatives of all countries and geared to the establishment of a new international economic order, would be genuine proof of a real desire to establish effective international co-operation for development.

IV

Importance of scientific, technological and cultural development

The establishment of a new international economic order is an all-embracing undertaking, in which consideration must be given to the various factors involved in development, and the way they interact. From this point of view, the importance of scientific, technological and socio-cultural factors needs to be stressed.

The modern applications of science and technology —particularly in the industrial field—are today the prerogative of the developed countries, which keep them more or less completely under their control, with a constant trend towards the devising of advanced techniques which, *ipso facto* give those countries power first in the technological, but also consequently, in the political and even military fields. In building up their economic potential, the industrialized countries have brought about considerable social changes and have become the vectors of a scientific and technological conception of the course of human development; the conviction has grown up that science, technology and development are indissolubly linked as cause and effect, resulting in a cumulative process which alone is capable—as it is generally believed among the developed countries—of meeting the needs which will be those of mankind at the end of the twentieth century.

It is true that science and its technological applications, which represent one of the great creative achievements of human genius, but not the only one, have helped in solving many problems connected with development, communications, the dissemination of knowledge and the improvement of standards of living. They have, however, given rise to other problems, particularly those arising from the changes brought about in society, the destruction of ancient cultures and the depreciation of other forms of knowledge; they have created new powers, at times concealed and uncontrolled, which have in certain cases, led to phenomena of domination between social categories and between nations. The spread of science and technology is not a neutral process; in point of fact, it has political, ideological and cultural implications. In a great many instances, it has come about haphazardly or on a basis of self-seeking, as regards both sectors of research and the communication of results.

Today, in the context of a new international economic order, 'What is needed is a new concept and long-range international strategy for the development of science and technology which reflects over-all global social needs—a concept and strategy that should not and must not, in their rational advance, become detached from the basic human orientation and fundamental values of human life' (Report of the Panel of Counsellors on Major World Problems).

Reflection on science and technology, which is, first and foremost, Unesco's responsibility within the United Nations system, is all the more important for the establishment of a new international economic order because the developing countries are behindhand in these two areas—a fact which prevents them from making the best use of their natural resources and human potential for development—and keenly conscious of their consequent dependence on the industrialized countries.

While they are seeking gradually to achieve the desired independence in this respect, many of them feel some misgiving about the scientific and technological models presented to them (methods of approach to truth, types of knowledge, process of harnessing resources). They are wondering whether modern science and, more especially, technology, are, as is claimed, really universally applicable, notwithstanding the fact that, for several centuries, they have originated in the West; whether the danger of compromising their own cultural identity or, in other words, their peoples' sense of the meaning of life, does not outweigh the results achieved or expected; and lastly, whether the reappraisal of old forms of knowledge and traditional techniques, long set aside or discredited by the invasion of industrial techniques, would not be both a counterbalance and a safeguard for their cultural identity, not to say simply for their liberty, as well as the most effective means of gaining the confidence and active participation of their people at large—not simply a technically trained élite—in a process of development to which all would contribute by their efforts and enterprise.

This shows sufficiently how important the development of science and technology is for the establishment of a new international economic order, and what is at stake in it. It explains why the United Nations General Assembly, at its Seventh Special Session (1975), regarded this as a vital area in which fruitful international co-operation for development purposes should be established among all Member States. The Assembly called for the study of a series of concrete proposals (Resolution 3362 (S-VII, Part III)) and invited all the relevant Agencies in the United Nations system, including Unesco, to take the necessary measures to this end. In particular it has provided for the holding in 1978 or 1979 of a United Nations Conference on Science and Technology for Development.

Science and technology
for development

Modern science has been directed to gaining greater knowledge of natural phenomena and to harnessing them to meet
man's needs. Man has, in fact, long been obliged to put up
with nature—climate, fauna and flora, epidemics—and has
had to struggle for survival with the help of elementary
techniques. Today the position is, as it were, reversed:
through his knowledge and techniques, man has gained
command over nature and its resources. After mastering and
developing the surface of the earth, he has explored and
exploited its substrata; he is now looking forward to the
prospects of making use of the ocean, the ocean floor and its
substrata—an immense reserve of resources as yet uniden-
tified—and the immediate or distant surroundings of the
earth (control of climate and solar energy). The relations
between man and nature have thus completely changed,
while instrumental techniques have become more complex
and more onerous; the direct contact between man and
nature reflected in the use of tools and empirical knowledge
has been replaced by lengthy processes of transformation,
interdependent operations, and sophisticated equipment.
Such is the basis proposed by modern science and technology, not merely for economic development, but for the
control of social phenomena (health, knowledge, communication, and so on).

Speculative, abstract science has gradually ceded its
place to the applied sciences; and today what people seem
most to need, to give purpose to their efforts and guide their
future, is reflection on the significance of things: the meaning
of life, of human endeavour, of communication and the very
will to exist (as individuals and as communities). The need,
then, for man to adapt himself to modern scientific knowledge is bringing back theoretical, philosophical or religious
inquiry to the place it had before; in the same way, history
and, with it, the various human sciences are acquiring a

sharper relevance. To know what kind of world to build, what type of men and women to produce for tomorrow, we must take due account of the origins of man and the stages he has already accomplished in the past. A new international order cannot be established solely on the basis of relatively short-range analyses, but must also be related to a view of the future that takes in man and societies, in all their dimensions and with all their manifold aspirations and needs. Yet only too often the political leaders, taken up by the demands of their office, no longer have the time for reflection or for discussion with all those who, through their activity, are brought to concern themselves with man and his destiny. In this respect, Unesco has a part to play.

The relationship between science and technology for the purposes of development is not a simple one. They do, in fact, interact. It is often the needs stemming from development and the perfecting of techniques that induce science to step up its research efforts and guide their direction. The process, moreover, comprises three logical, if not chronological, phases: fundamental research, applied research, and development. Today fundamental research, although essential in the long run, is in danger of being somewhat neglected in favour of applied research and development. Failure to recognize a social and even political function in fundamental research would be regrettable, even if its immediate usefulness is not apparent. It forms part of culture, as poetry and ethics have done.

The fact that a scientific foundation is vital to development raises an ethical question: are the discoverers of scientific knowledge—whether individuals or nations—entitled to appropriate that knowledge as their exclusive right? No doubt such knowledge is increasingly obtained through the work of research teams, assisted moreover by a favourable infrastructure (laboratories, apparatus, communications) and by the combination of efforts. But should it not be made available to the rest of mankind by publication and through appropriate institutions? Even though competition may have a stimulating effect, it is quite wrong, when the vast needs of the nations are considered, that research work should be duplicated because of narrow national particularism. What we have to do is to administer this common heritage of mankind and enrich it for the benefit of all. It is vital to have a world strategy for scientific research which will have regard for sectoral and geographical distribution. It would indeed be a pity if certain branches of human knowledge were allowed to die out because they are not of immediate interest, and if the present geographical concentration of the finest brains in a few zones equipped with more modern facilities which, coupled with high remuneration, exert a power of attraction, were to continue. This phenomenon of the concentration of intellect in certain privileged centres of scientific research (regardless of the nationality of the research workers) results in the impoverishment of the other regions, which are pushed out to the periphery; this has often been denounced by the developing countries. The individual research specialist must no doubt be left a certain freedom which is conducive to creativity; creativity probably often stems from the contagious effects of team-work among specialists. It might also perhaps be argued that this phenomenon foreshadows possible transnational developments for the future. But the fact still remains that certain nations are seriously impoverished by it. Any solution will, of course, have to take account of the motivations of researchers and perhaps seek to turn them in the direction of putting service to others, to the people as a whole, their nations and mankind in first place. Measures might be suggested by the competent Specialized Agencies and more particularly by Unesco, with a view to promoting a fairer regional distribution of talents.

The general direction followed by research and its technological applications is connected with the social system chosen by each nation. Some countries have adopted a liberal policy, especially in regard to applied research, leaving it to private bodies (business firms, laboratories, hospital centres) to determine the lines of inquiry to which such work is to be addressed. Others have a more centralized policy. At all events, one determining factor is the way research is financed; a great many lines of research depend on the amount of resources available, on those in control of such resources, and on their aims. From this point of view, it may be regretted that the means at the disposal of United Nations Agencies for the promotion and encouragement of research are still slender in comparison with the resources available to the developed countries. It is also to be noted that a large proportion of research in the developed countries is directed towards exclusively military and national production ends. This is a self-centred attitude that the developing countries regret: 'the developed countries should . . . increase substantially the proportion of their research and development devoted to specific problems of primary interest to the developing countries' (Resolution 3362 (S-VII, Part III, para. 2)).

It would be useful, for deciding on the direction to be followed in scientific activities, to make an appraisal balancing the credit side (advantages) against the debit side (dangers and cost) of the research undertaken and the results achieved (before considering their application). An attempt might well be made—and Unesco could take the initiative in this—by means of wide-ranging public discussions, to establish a programme of research priorities which appear to be the most pressing for the well-being of mankind, and to submit it to the nations. This might also be one of the aims to set for the United Nations Conference on Science and Technology for Development, which is planned for 1978 or 1979. Unesco would also have a part to play as regards the study of possible future trends and joint consultation.

Unesco should pay particular attention to strengthening the links between the natural and the social sciences for the definition of appropriate strategies. 'Science is a product of history and of society, and it owes just as much to the social environment as to the work of the scientists. . . . A concept of science, based on an analysis of the interactions between science and society, would result in the formulation of strategies comprising new priorities related to social progress and the solution of the major world problems; it would also encourage the developing countries to work out their own scientific and technical development strategies. Moreover, each step forward in the natural sciences should be accompanied by a corresponding advance in the social sciences. There can be no question of stopping or slowing down the progress of science; on the contrary, it must be harnessed to the task of solving the most serious problems which confront us.' (Report of the Panel of Counsellors on Major World Problems.)

Unesco's endeavours should be focused more especially on the relations between science, technology, the satisfaction of human needs and the evolution of society. The failure to appreciate some of man's deepest aspirations, which is reflected in the subjection of science and technology to unreasoned and destructive ends or, more simply, to the mere satisfaction—not even equitably from the geopolitical point of view—of short-term material needs, has brought about situations in this respect which are sometimes tragic and always fraught with peril for the future. The community of nations must therefore make urgent efforts to remedy this state of affairs in the context of a process of reflection on the future development of mankind appropriate to the growing consciousness of world solidarity from which the idea of a new economic order has emerged. As the Panel of Counsellors on Major World Problems has rightly pointed out: 'A truly sound concept of the future of contemporary civilization can only be based on a parallel development of man and society, on the one hand, and technology, on the other. We are entering a period in which—without well thought-out programmes of social development, without a purposeful control of social processes and without a purposeful shaping of the way of life—man's socially useful abilities will be prodigally wasted. We need to realize that the control of social processes is at once the most comprehensive and the most difficult task confronting contemporary science.' (Report of the Panel of Counsellors on Major World Problems.)

Modern science—in the areas of physics, chemistry, biology and even meteorology—represents a formidable power that can be directed towards progress or towards destruction. Identification of this power at the international and national levels, the establishment of procedures for its guidance and control, and the formulation of a number of ethical rules for its use, are all clearly necessary measures to clarify the situation with a view to development and peace.

The possibilities afforded by technology for changing the nature of development, its trend and its objectives are such that those who hold the keys of technology often also hold those of economic development. The technical factor can no longer be regarded merely as a component of the production process; it has become one of the main agents of change. In such a context, it may be wondered whether appropriation of the instruments of technology by private or national authorities, and the direction of the course of research and development by private interests, should not give way to a policy of social control. Should not the concept of private ownership as applied to areas of knowledge be revised, and should not technology be regarded as an asset whose administration and direction should be primarily determined by social and human objectives?

At the national level, the material, political and cultural infrastructures necessary for scientific and technological development need to be established—or strengthened—so that each nation may: (a) participate in the general advance of knowledge and thus enlarge its contribution to the activities of the international scientific community; identify the scientific and technical problems that hamper its development; select and adapt the types of knowledge and know-how, which it seems desirable to acquire by transfer in the context of the national science and technology policy; (b) develop the necessary machinery for promoting the flow of scientific and technological information and the transfer of knowledge, and strengthen the links between its own machinery and the corresponding international and regional machinery; and (c) develop, at all levels, scientific and technological training proper.

The developing countries and the transfer of science and technology: growth of the scientific and technological potential of the developing countries

The speeding up of the growth of the scientific and technological potential of the developing countries is, from all points of view, an urgent necessity. While the importance of increasing the fundamental research potential, linked with the development of higher education, must not be neglected, attention must also be directed to the practical objectives of medium- and long-term development, and more systematic programming must be introduced.

For a developing country, it is essential that a national scientific and technological infrastructure should be established if it is gradually to achieve more autonomous development, to gain greater international independence, and to safeguard its cultural individuality and sovereignty more effectively.

The establishment of an academically dominated scientific infrastructure—which is relatively common—could, if we are not careful, lead to an 'élitist' attitude and neglect of the simple technologies adapted to present development needs. In order to avoid any possible dichotomy, the process of implanting scientific thought in developing countries should begin at the bottom of the pyramid as well as at the top, especially if we really want to develop natural and human resources for the good of the whole population (and not of an élite more or less closely linked with foreign countries). The élitist tendency of any scientific institution is, incidentally, reflected in the emphasis on centralization, the establishment of fully integrated networks, control of operations at all stages, and non-participation by the consumer or the producer. It is often taken for granted in developing countries that there is no capacity for innovation among the average ordinary citizens; but this state of affairs is probably to be attributed to the technological impact of the major systems, which have never allowed the weaker systems either the time or the means to finance their own operations.

We must put our trust in the inventive power of the ordinary people and give them both the means to try out their new ideas, and the self-confidence without which success is impossible. In this way, a country's capacity to absorb science and technology can be gradually and harmoniously developed. What is more, native creativity and the ability to assimilate foreign technologies correctly are closely associated; the two attitudes are complementary. In the sphere of health, for example, we have seen that, after ambitious programmes and optimum standards of efficiency (so many doctors for so many inhabitants) have been drawn up, it has been thought well to recommend the establishment of a medical network based on 'bare-foot doctors' who have had a simpler, more practical training, working among the people and familiar with their real needs; a similar line of development might accordingly be recommended for production systems, more particularly in agriculture and for certain types of industry. The question of creating an indigenous scientific potential is worth considering closely. In the medical sciences and pharmacology, indigenous science is already being rehabilitated, although advanced technology in these fields is not rejected either. In agriculture and animal husbandry, traditional systems are being re-examined in an effort to find means of solving certain problems concerning water and soil. This respect for a past hitherto rejected represents the beginning of a new kind of wisdom which goes back to first principles for the study of the development of man's relationship with the natural environment, a relationship at one and the same time of domination and adaptation.

A non-aggressive modern technology can re-establish relations with the traditional system. Similarly, one of the reasons why small farming units seem better able to achieve a really satisfactory combination of natural production factors with others brought in from abroad, lies in their capacity for innovation, which enables them to meet the challenges of nature by drawing both on their own experience and on the new data provided by science. This optimum dimension, this level at which science and experience can be effectively combined, must be discovered in the industrial as well as in the agricultural sphere, with all due regard for particular local conditions.

A broad, deep area of human capacity will thus be developed, equipped to produce its own innovations and to receive foreign technological and scientific contributions, adapting them to local needs.

Conditions for the transfer of technologies
from developed to developing countries

In the Declaration on the Establishment of a New International Economic Order, the Member States agreed on the following principle: 'giving to the developing countries access to the achievements of modern science and technology, and promoting the transfer of technology and the creation of indigenous technology for the benefit of the developing countries in forms and in accordance with procedures which are suited to their economies'. (Resolution 3201 (S-VI, para. 4 (p)).) This principle was first put into practice in the Programme of Action with regard to the transfer of technology (Resolution 3202 (S-VI, Part IV)) and in Part III, 'Science and Technology', of Resolution 3362 (S-VII), adopted by the United Nations General Assembly at its Seventh Special Session.

First, the transfer of technology, as a modern form of international exchange, is of particular importance when it is a question of transferring technologies from industrialized to developing countries, on account of the needs of the latter and the technical superiority of the former and, above all, of the lack of reciprocity in this exchange. The idea, now widely accepted, of 'technology transfer' covers a complex set of factors, not only technological (methods of processing raw materials, management and social organization), but economic, political and cultural as well. We must be able to identify and distinguish the various levels of technical expression and application (patents and licences, know-how, show-how) as well as the different transmission channels (documents, experts, setting up of companies and, above all, training). From the economic standpoint, the transfer of technology to developing countries often gives rise to trade practices which are detrimental to the buyer-countries. Efforts should be made to achieve greater equity (by fixing fair prices and securing greater transparency of the market): 'All efforts should be made . . . to adapt commercial practices governing transfer of technology to the requirements of developing countries and to prevent abuse of the rights of sellers'. (Resolution 3202 (S-VI, Part IV (d)).) Similarly: 'Developed countries should improve the transparency of the industrial property market in order to facilitate the technological choices of developing countries' (Resolution 3362 (S-VII, Part III, para. 6)). In the last resort, consideration might even be given to the possibility of free 'transfer' of any technology which could be speedily adapted and might be of assistance in redressing the most glaring inequalities.

Although Unesco is concerned with this form of technological exchange from the point of view of securing greater justice, the Organization has a more specific part to play with regard to the socio-cultural aspects.

Second, the problem of the transfer of technology is, of course, by no means new. The history of civilizations is concerned, in part, with retracing the ways and means whereby certain technical discoveries as vitally important as fire, the rudder, the wheel and the clock spread out to other peoples from the places where they were made. Recent historical studies have begun an analysis of the transfer of techniques from one country to another in the nineteenth century, and from one socio-economic area to another during the spread of industrialization in the West. Such consideration of recent experience may usefully be continued. At the present time, the transfer of technology to the developing countries is unprecedented in its scope, rapidity and urgency, and implies such radical changes, that some countries regard it, on the one hand as a necessity for meeting the needs of their people more quickly and, on the other, as a form of cultural aggression, bringing about far-reaching changes in their methods of work, ways of thinking, patterns of consumption and system of social relationships and values. There is also a risk of breaking up the fabric of society and the human environment: alongside centres or sectors which are assimilating modern technology—and, incidentally, liable to form 'technological isolates'—there will be broad strata of the population or whole regions cut off from the mainstream of technology or drawing on it only through the medium of a few consumer goods.

The transfer of technology calls for careful study of the best conditions and the effects of this spread of knowledge. This is a matter which must receive attention from Unesco, and reference may be made to some of the avenues to which research might be directed.

Third, an analysis of the time factor is essential in order to decide on the best policies for the reception of foreign technologies and the mobilization of material and intellectual resources (both national and international). The true factor is principally of importance in two respects:

What priorities and what degree of urgency should be allotted to the various possible and desirable development objectives? What limiting factors will be encountered? What are the technologies which may make it possible to neutralize the effects of such limiting factors and to attain these objectives?

How quickly can technologies be introduced into a country

(economic dissemination) and how soon can the indigenous population assimilate them properly, in such a way as to have full command of them and derive maximum benefit from them (cultural dissemination)? In agriculture, for instance, the doubling of the production of the developing countries in order to meet the needs of an ever-increasing population does not, on the most favourable assumptions—i.e. with a regular annual growth rate of 3 per cent—seem likely to be achieved until the end of the century. It is in fact not only a question of technological transfers (machines, fertilizers, irrigation systems, new seeds, etc.), but also of adapting modern systems to a wide variety of social and ecological conditions, which calls for a dynamic combination of scientific analysis and action in the field; the human potential of the regions concerned must be able to assimilate this technology, which cannot, without ill-effects, be imposed as an alien factor, bound inevitably to upset the balance.

The same is true in the industrial sphere. The developing countries are anxious to force events and make up lost time to some extent, so as to achieve the over-all target set in March 1975 at the second session of the General Conference of the United Nations Industrial Development Organization (by the year 2000, the developing countries should have at least 25 per cent of world manufacturing production); that is an ambitious, albeit entirely justified, objective, but it presupposes a determined pursuit of efficiency, which would rule out any possibility of a slow ripening, starting from the country's own basic conditions, which would gradually result in a process of innovation and adaptation coming from within. This, then, would represent the use on a large scale of existing technological capital.

These two examples show that the time we have is short; in fact it is limited to one generation. In practical terms, the present generation is responsible for the political, economic and financial conditions in which a more or less massive transfer can be made; the following generation—which is now beginning to play an active part in the working world—will have, within ten or twenty years, to absorb the impact of this transfer and gain control over its technical and social consequences.

In the face of such urgent problems, fundamental research projects on a global scale, dealing for example with the relations between man and his environment, between man and the biosphere, or the genetic future of the human race, are liable, despite their undoubted interest, to be pushed into the background, not without harmful effects.

The double sense of urgency attached to industrialization and the massive increase of agricultural production may well lead to neglect of the ecological and socio-economic factors which constitute basic constraints. These constraints can only be advantageously removed by rational policies, i.e. policies based on scientific research. Unesco, whose essential responsibility is to safeguard and promote the socio-cultural values of humanity, has a special part to play by helping developing countries to establish a sound scientific basis for such policies.

What we have to do, in fact, is to incorporate science and technology into the general system of cultural and social values: and it is from this point of view that the transfer of technology should be studied. It must be emphasized, however, that Member States themselves will have to work out their own means of achieving this dynamic integration in the light of their national circumstances and the particular constraints that they impose.

Fourth, if we are to speed up the transfer of technology and thus help in solving urgent development problems, it must be possible to rely on local transmission centres able not only to receive information but also to provide information in the other direction—as clearly and fully as possible—on the local conditions and limiting factors which slow down the possible application of scientific concepts and technological processes. 'It is therefore a task of the utmost importance and urgency to establish everywhere the local

bases of real scientific development, that is to say, to constitute, maintain and animate an indigenous scientific potential,
establishing and widening as many contacts as possible with
the people around it.' (Report of the Panel of Counsellors on
Major World Problems.) The 'élitist' approach to the transfer
of science and technology must therefore be abandoned in
favour of developing a broader foundation marked by an
intimate familiarity with local problems, which will play an
active part not only in receiving information but also in
providing it and in raising new questions. This is a prerequisite for the success of any such transfer, especially as an
'élitist' conception of the scientific establishment is liable to
result in loss of contact with the fundamental needs of the
population at large.

Again, the scientific and technological systems of the
industrialized countries have grown in complication and in
scope. Such global-scale, high-technology, macro-systems
are not, themselves, suited to dealing with the real needs of
the masses, but should be connected up to technological
micro-systems designed for meeting needs in the essential
areas of food, housing, education and health.

Production macro-systems, both in agriculture and in
industry, may well spread all over the world, for considerations of speed and efficiency, and react on the existing
micro-systems. They are now preponderant in international
economic relations and hamper the development of the
micro-systems. A change must be brought about, so that
each developing country may be able to take full advantage
of its natural resources in the context of a closely knit international economy, without being subject to pressure from the
existing industrial and commercial macro-systems. The sovereignty which each State exercises over its natural resources
consists not so much in the appropriation of those resources
in the interests of national economic self-sufficiency, as in
the right to make the best use of them in appropriate and
effective conditions, at national and international level.

Finally, the transfer of technology should also cover its

adaptation to the economic and socio-cultural conditions of the receiving countries. Such adaptation implies a thorough knowledge of the country's needs and the cast of mind and capacity for work of its people, as well as of its material and climatic conditions. It also includes appropriate forms of training.

Other possibilities besides adaptation are beginning to open up, such as that of alternative (or so-called 'soft') technology. It is, of course, true that in both cases—in adapted (or appropriate) technology and alternative technology—certain criteria are the same: maximum economy of energy, better use of human labour, adaptation of the scale of production to small communities, maximum reduction of the restrictive factors in the competitive market. The main ideas behind alternative technologies—which imply considerations of autonomy—derive, however, from other points of view: regional autonomy, conservation of natural resources, direct control by producers and consumers, absence of exploitation, ecological stability and job-satisfaction in the production process. The basis of alternative technology is self-sufficiency and self-management. It represents one of the aspects of an alternative policy which tends ultimately towards almost complete national economic self-sufficiency and runs counter to a policy of free communication and fuller technological and scientific interpenetration.

These themes can usefully be studied with care to see what they hold in the way of aspirations and possible achievements, and what place would then fall to international co-operation.

International co-operation

The application of science and technology to development is one of the principal areas of international co-operation contemplated by the United Nations General Assembly at its Sixth and Seventh Special Sessions.

This co-operation has three aspects: co-operation among developing countries at the regional and subregional levels; co-operation between developed and developing countries; the role of international agencies, in particular those of the United Nations system.

These three aspects are complementary and must be regarded as interlocking, rather than as competing with one another. They should be the subject of flexible medium-term planning, with an eye to the more distant future. The corresponding measures for the establishment of new institutions should take account of the need to avoid duplication and hence to begin by carrying out a critical evaluation of existing bodies, their efficiency, and their ability to adapt to the requirements of a new international economic order. The basic assumptions of the current programmes should also be revised: they are often no longer valid because it is now realized that more urgent needs exist and because a new approach to development and to international relations has emerged. So far as institutions are concerned, we must also avoid the error of thinking that a problem is solved once it has been decided to set up a new agency. Furthermore, rigidity and bureaucratization must at all costs be avoided, since the object is to see that institutions have the necessary capacity to adapt themselves to dealing with new sets of problems.

If Unesco's contribution to the establishment of a new international economic order in the field of science is to be improved, the Secretariat will have to consider the possibility of reorganizing its activities along three main lines: (a) 'evaluation and forward planning', in order to make a realistic reappraisal of programming and of the phasing of the different programmes according to their probable impact on specific situations; (b) 'scientific and technological alternatives', in order to see how technologies from outside can be adapted to meeting the specific needs of each region according to its ecological and human characteristics and— as a parallel and complementary theme—how the inherent innovative capacities of the local communities can be stimulated; and (c) 'information in the service of development', in order to review the different types of exchange of information, and of interpersonal and international communication, in terms of their possible impact on development policies.

Various proposals relating to international co-operation, at different levels, were put forward in the Lima Programme (Conference of Ministers for Foreign Affairs of Non-Aligned Countries, August 1975) and at the Seventh Special Session of the United Nations General Assembly (September 1975).

Scientific and technical co-operation among developing countries

A programme of scientific and technical co-operation among developing countries is to be agreed upon by the countries concerned, by March 1976, and will take practical form in the establishment of a centre responsible for promoting such co-operation and in a common strategy for developing countries in regard to science and technology.

While deciding to lay down the necessary bases for the development of an effective, viable national technology, the developing countries are considering the establishment of technology transfer centres in order, through exchanges, to increase their capacity for carrying out complex technological processes. Furthermore, the developing countries have agreed to encourage the establishment of advisory organizations at national and other levels and, as far as possible, to approach these organizations first.

Co-operation between developed and developing countries

The United Nations General Assembly decided, at its Seventh Special Session, that to assist in the development of the scientific and technological infrastructure of developing countries, developed countries should contribute to the establishment of an industrial technological information bank and consider the possibility of regional and sectoral banks, in order to make available a greater flow to developing countries of information permitting a more enlightened selection of technologies, in particular advanced technologies.

The developed countries should also expand their assistance to developing countries for the direct financing of their science and technology programmes, besides increasing substantially the proportion of their research and development devoted to specific problems of primary interest to developing countries.

Furthermore, developed countries should facilitate access by developing countries to informatics and relevant technical information. Inasmuch as in market economies advanced technologies with respect to industrial production are most frequently developed by private institutions, developed countries should assist and encourage those institutions in providing effective technologies in support of the priorities of developing countries.

Lastly, developed countries should give developing countries the freest and fullest possible access to technologies whose transfer is not subject to private decision.

Co-operation among international organizations

Efforts should be made to evolve an international code of conduct for the transfer of technology, corresponding in particular to the needs of the developing countries; with a view to its adoption by States.

The international conventions on patents and trademarks should be revised in the light of the special needs of developing countries.

The United Nations Conference on Science and Technology for Development, which is to be held in 1978 or 1979, will aim mainly at strengthening the technological capacity of developing countries to enable them to apply science and technology to their own development.

The United Nations General Assembly, at its thirty-first

session, will consider the possibility of setting up within the United Nations system an international energy institute to assist all developing countries in research and development on energy resources.

The competent bodies of the United Nations, and in particular Unesco, should give high priority to work aimed at facilitating the transfer and diffusion of technology. Steps should be taken to ensure that the technology and experience available within the United Nations system is widely disseminated and readily available to developing countries in need of it.

Some priority challenges

Scientific and technical research and the transfer of technologies for the purposes of development should be directed first and foremost to meeting three challenges which have now become the subject of world-wide concern: the challenge of eradicating hunger and overcoming poverty; the challenge of energy; the challenge of a more equitable distribution of productive capacity and employment openings.

The struggle against poverty

The challenge of poverty covers three particularly urgent problems: hunger, illiteracy and disease.

The World Food Conference (November 1974) stressed the present and future extent of the food problem; world agricultural production must be increased and distributed more equitably—an essential step without which there can be no question of a new international economic order. International co-operation is of major importance, as are the use of appropriate technologies and the acceleration of scientific research in these vitally necessary fields. Emphasis must be placed on integrated rural development and the reconstitution of a rural society which will be conscious of its mission, properly trained for modern production tasks and will have its status improved in relation to other social groups. In developing countries where there is still a large peasant population, often neglected in comparison with the urban areas (health facilities and cultural infrastructure, standards of living, etc.), and without many of the basic administrative and social services, the drift away from the country areas, which leads to over-population of the towns, to the formation of an urban proletariat and often to a fall in agricultural production, must be reversed. People have, incidentally, been well aware of this sort of problem for quite a long time; what is needed is that it should be translated into terms of policy and programme objectives, specifying the place to be given to investment—both social (education, health) and economic and institutional—to support a dynamic revival of the rural communities. It will also be advisable to determine, with due regard to the sociological and ecological context, the various types of transfers of knowledge and technology and, above all, the type of cultural promotion work which should go with such investment. The respective importance of the factors involved does not seem so far to have been studied in sufficient depth, as the emphasis has been rather on the quantitative aspect of the food resources needed, whereas the question of restoring and revitalizing a human environment by giving its inhabitants fresh confidence in their own possibilities and in the quality of their life also needs attention. The economic aspect, being the more urgent, has bulked much larger than the socio-cultural aspect, which is nevertheless essential from the human point of view and from that of long-term efficacy.

A fairer distribution of income within the nation, to the advantage of the rural population, and a more balanced distribution of agricultural income itself, are among the essential conditions for the establishment of a new international economic order. Whenever new techniques, however elementary, are introduced into a social environment where inequalities are rife, there is a danger of making those inequalities worse unless special measures are taken. Where the use of new high-yield varieties is concerned, for example, experience has shown that the small farmer has neither the minimum training nor the necessary means to take advantage of them; he cannot participate in the change, and the innovation merely benefits the richer people. This inequality of opportunity for sharing in innovation should therefore be borne in mind and appropriate steps taken to reduce it.

Education, more especially in rural areas, remains a challenge for the future, which, far from diminishing as the years pass, is becoming more serious on account of population growth; there is a threshold of poverty in this respect, with very great inequalities between countries, which must be overcome.

Assuming that the population growth rates, on the one hand, and school enrolment rates, on the other, continue to be similar throughout the 1970s to what they were during the 1960s, it may be estimated that, by 1980, the number of children between 5 and 14 years of age who will not receive schooling will reach 240 million, while the total of adult illiterates will be 820 million (for a total population of approximately 4,500 million); the majority of them will be found in the developing countries.

In the twenty-five least-developed countries, where the annual *per capita* income is less than $150, the illiteracy rates are generally above 80 per cent; and it is in these same countries that the education systems and out-of-school education programmes are least effective.

Illiteracy, which is a logical consequence of poverty, is slowing up development, and particularly agricultural production, just because it prevents any substantial broadening of knowledge.

Lastly—although this is a question which does not come directly within Unesco's field of competence—mention must be made of the tragic importance of health problems in developing countries. Through the combined effects of malnutrition, which in very serious cases has an irremediable adverse effect on the development of children's brains, and of diseases which, in many cases, could be quite easily cured, or even totally eliminated by the use of inexpensive means provided by modern medicine, the people who most need to put forth all their efforts to struggle free from poverty are physiologically unable to do so. Here again, the mobilization of all the means available, better organization, and perhaps most of all educational action, are absolutely essential.

Energy

The history of the economic development of civilizations is also that of the control of energy in its different forms. Our thinking about the establishment of a new international economic order has been prompted, from the political as well as from the economic point of view, by what has come to be termed the 'oil crisis'. This has brought about a readjustment in the balance of power and of capital but has also led to an active search for other forms of potential energy for the future, while a campaign against waste is now under way. The structural relations of industries have been disrupted, along with relative prices and trade. The disturbance (accompanied by changes in the prices of raw materials) has affected the production of food and consumer goods, services and even the day-to-day functioning of urban and rural societies; oil is both a raw material and a source of energy. The developing countries which import oil, raw materials for industry and capital goods have been very severely hit, sometimes to a catastrophic extent, by the economic upheaval of the past two years. Besides the emergency measures that must be applied, the foundations for longer-term economic and technological solutions need to be laid, as otherwise the economies of the countries which do not have so-called 'conventional' energy resources are liable to be doomed never to achieve a sufficient degree of independence. Economic collective security, as the corollary of a new economic order, requires that each developing country should be able to formulate an energy policy of its own, drawing, if necessary, upon non-conventional resources. This is particularly important because the distribution of energy in great areas of non-urbanized country where communications and climatic conditions are difficult, represents a major problem for balanced regional development in many developing countries. The poverty of rural areas is also partly due to the difficulty of providing energy and knowing how to use it properly.

Many countries in tropical and subtropical regions could make use of non-conventional sources of energy (solar energy, wind power) which we know how to harness, although their applications in specific environments, and the investments required, have not yet been studied in sufficient detail.

While the United Nations system has already embarked on studies on the various forms of energy, these are still on a more or less piecemeal basis and there has been no combined effort to apply the results of science and technology to the most needy countries in this sphere. The time seems to have come to undertake an intergovernmental programme on energy, in liaison with the other objectives of integrated development.

Distribution of industrial productive capacity

What is needed here is to encourage a more equitable and rational distribution, among groups of countries, of the production of the principal goods and services.

The second General Conference of the United Nations Industrial Development Organization (March 1975) and the United Nations General Assembly at its Seventh Special Session (Resolution 3362 (S-VII, Part IV)) set out the conditions for a strategy for the redeployment of industries that would enable the developing countries to play a more important part in world industrial production, including basic industries and capital goods industries. The Lima Declaration and Plan of Action on Industrial Development and Co-operation give priority to the need to close the widening gap between the industrial potential of the industrialized nations and of the developing countries, and constitute a challenge, having regard to the extent of the effort to be made and the difficulty in co-ordinating all possible means to arrive at the figure of 25 per cent by the year 2000 (share of the developing countries in world industrial production).

This rapid advance of industrialization will provide a solution, in some small measure, to the very serious problem of lack of employment openings and the consequent likelihood of unemployment for many young people. This problem, which is already evident in many developing countries and is aggravated by the world economic crisis, will inevitably worsen during the next decade to the point of catastrophe unless technical research into production and working procedures is undertaken in order to correct the situation a little. The World Employment Conference to be held in 1976 will endeavour to assess the extent of the task and to suggest possible courses of action.

Rapid industrialization presupposes an educational system geared to the training of the executives, technicians and workers required. This will, in many cases, involve a fairly comprehensive reform of curricula and teaching methods, for which Unesco should provide the benefit of its experience.

The social and cultural effects of such high-speed industrialization will also have to be assessed with a view to mitigating them. It would no doubt be rash, from the human standpoint, to embark—without properly appreciating all the implications—on forms of action likely to upset social relations and systems of values, when these are based on an effective community of interests that safeguards the dignity of labour and of the worker. Moreover, the solution to the problem of full employment concerns the industrial sector just as much as the rural sector whose potentialities are still not used to the full.

Other challenges are already looming around the year 2000: a genetic challenge, a population challenge, pollution and destruction of the environment, urban overcrowding, inflation of information and knowledge. If they are not taken up in time, they could endanger the new international economic order that the nations will have striven to establish over the years from 1975 to 1985. They are all the result of scientific and technological development. In the interests of mankind as a whole, the time has come for active measures to secure better concerted national science policies and to direct them to promoting the well-being of the world community. The organizations in the United Nations system are directly concerned in this concerted action and the most important non-governmental organizations should be associated with it.

V

Unesco's contribution

Mention has frequently been made in the preceding pages of the part which Unesco should play, within its fields of competence, in research and activities directed towards the establishment of a new international economic order. At this point it will be well to say something of certain areas in which such action could be taken, under the terms of Resolution 12.1 adopted by the General Conference at its eighteenth session, on the basis of the principles of endogenous progress, international co-operation and social justice.

Unesco's role would be a peripheral one if a new international order could be established merely by transforming—even radically transforming—the economic relationships which at present exist between industrialized and developing countries. Such a transformation is imperative, but it cannot of itself bring about, a more extensive change in political, social and cultural factors, with a view to integrated development. Unesco's role has its place in this over-all plan, and Unesco's tasks in particular will be: to contribute to the laying of the scientific and technological foundations which will enable every country to make better use of its natural resources; to broaden the scope of education and direct its course so that the people of each country will be better fitted to see to their own development; to develop communications and information systems; and through the development of the social sciences, to stimulate self-examination in every society in order to help it to derive the greatest advantage from the instruments of change, whilst not losing its own identity.

Construction of the scientific and technological foundations which will enable every country to make better use of its natural resources

The aim of Unesco's natural science activities, in the context of a new economic and social order, is to make the most of existing and potential human and material wealth so that it can benefit the greatest number, both people now alive and, above all, future generations.

Unesco's activities, generally speaking, have a dual aspect: on the one hand, international co-operation for the development of knowledge (intergovernmental research programmes) and, on the other, action to improve Member States' ability to solve their own problems in these fields, by helping them either to work out scientific policies which meet national needs or, as part of their operational activities, to train scientists and engineers and to develop institutions and programmes for study and research.

In ecology, the intergovernmental and interdisciplinary Programme on Man and the Biosphere (MAB) is designed to develop an integrated and practical approach in the study of man's relationships with his environment in the different ecosystems, including urban ecosystems. It calls for close co-operation between natural scientists and specialists in the humanities. Another aim of this programme is to train specialists and to establish the institutions needed by

Member States for work in ecology, soil science and the earth's natural resources.

The International Hydrological Programme (IHP) is concerned with problems relating to both the quantity and the quality of water. It provides Member States with information and with opportunities for training.

The International Geological Correlation Programme is intended to provide the bases for a better knowledge of the geology of the planet and its formations so that we may have a better understanding of the origin and distribution of mineral resources. International geological maps, which are needed for research and teaching, are drawn and prepared for publication. The study of natural risks (e.g. drought, floods, climatic disturbances and earthquakes) and of preventive measures is actively pursued.

With regard to the sea's resources of various kinds, which are of growing importance for many developing countries, the Intergovernmental Oceanographic Commission, through its programmes and scientific services, ensures that nations co-operate on a large scale in the study of the oceans; and the Organization helps countries to take a more active part in these programmes and to tackle their marine and coastal problems.

This scientific contribution on a world-wide scale should help States to increase their ability to identify and tackle their own problems by themselves. Experience of the implementation of these intergovernmental programmes shows that, even at the initial stage of the co-ordination of research, when development is not immediately involved, the work of co-ordination requires sustained attention, although the scientists and specialists concerned have a basis of fellowship and interests in common. The most modern satellite-based techniques for inventorying natural resources require to be co-ordinated by local organizations for which the national authorities are responsible. Although the world-wide approach is essential, it is in no way a substitute for national and local efforts to transform the environment, and even less is it a substitute for the elaboration of a suitable technology which will permit the best possible use to be made of natural and human resources, within the framework of systems which have their own ecological and human characteristics.

Every nation should direct its efforts towards the establishment of suitable institutions for research proper and for the adaptation of knowledge and procedures whose acquisition by transfer seems justified in the context of the nation's scientific and technological policy. A higher and technical education infrastructure will make it possible to train research workers, engineers and technologists, encouraging them to work with originality and to apply their findings in ways connected with fundamental research and the needs of national production (agricultural and industrial).

Ways of broadening the scope of education and directing its course so that the people of each country will be fitted to see to their own development

The establishment of a new and more equitable international economic order implies changes in the education systems of many developing countries. For in many cases, through lack of sufficient resources, most adults and many young people are refused access to education and information and do not receive the minimum of training. In many cases, too, existing education systems are expensive copies of systems developed in industrialized countries, and must be radically changed to take account of the cultural situations, so that the knowledge and the know-how needed for agricultural and industrial development can be acquired.

Unesco's activities in the field of education lie within this framework of change. There is a level of poverty which we must rise above. To educate people to produce and so, through their own activities, to satisfy essential requirements with regard to food, clothing, housing and health is a form of struggle against poverty from both the material and the psychological point of view. Instead of adopting a fatalistic attitude towards poverty, the individual and the community will feel responsible for their own development, glimpsing objectives which they can themselves decide on and acquiring means by which to reach them. This growing realization of their capabilities will be a powerful motivation and, to enable them to reach this stage, the following activities could be undertaken in co-operation with the various countries:

The preparation of educational policies which will make it possible to align education with the general development effort.

The remodelling of present educational systems so that they take greater account of the economic, social and cultural realities of each country. They should, in particular, make it possible to train men and women who have their roots in their environment, but who are able to stimulate the changes necessary for the progress of all the communities to which they belong.

The preparation of formal and non-formal, school and out-of-school curricula which will enable all to acquire techniques which will be of use to them in their work, whilst developing their ability to take the initiative and to change.

The linking of productive work with education so as to (a) contribute to character training and to the acquisition of manual skills by upgrading manual work, seen as a vital part of the integral training of young people; (b) associate schoolchildren and students, as producers, with the country's economic and social development programmes, so that they will be able, through their work, to provide some of the resources necessary for their own subsistence; (c) develop closer links between intellectual and manual workers (labourers and peasants), since the convergence of their efforts in mutual understanding is essential to national development. In the least developed countries—one might even say in all countries—an abstract, bookish and alienating kind of education, an education which has little to do with the specific nature of society, contributes little to development.

The encouragement of education services which, at the higher level, possess centres of excellence that train research workers, technical experts and other vital specialists, but, with the maintenance of a constant link between research, training and production.

The establishment of machinery to ensure the integration of these changes with changes occurring in other sectors of society.

The problem of illiteracy is so great that the establishment of a new economic order implies its eradication. Illiteracy is a brake on development and restricts human rights.

For this reason, Unesco is striving to promote the participation of people at large in development activities as part of functional literacy and adult education programmes, co-operative movements and action to improve the status of peasants, and by providing information, through the mass media, about development (health, hygiene, nutrition, craft work and agricultural techniques). Unesco is also contributing to: (a) improving the effectiveness of the educational system by using structures linked with development, promoting the training of teachers and using suitable methods and equipment; (b) planning and administering education at national and local level and intensifying research and development activities.

If these complex and independent tasks are to be successfully accomplished, orders of priority in national plans must be established.

Development of communications and information systems

Under its Constitution, part of Unesco's task is to promote the free flow of ideas, which implies the free flow of information. Despite the advance of technology, however, many countries are still without elementary facilities for transmitting and receiving information and ideas. The scarcity of equipment and qualified staff in the developing countries is felt all the more keenly in that the modern media of information offer greater possibilities of hastening the progress of education, spreading scientific and technological knowledge, and promoting development.

Operating on a world-wide scale, some information agencies—most of which have their headquarters in one of the industrialized countries—have, by reason of their equipment and capital, acquired a position of strength which probably enables them to offer better services but also leads them to convey one-way information reflecting the point of view of those countries, and which, above all, allows them to dominate the information market to an extent that borders on cultural aggression. Only a few powerful countries and—what is more serious—a few transnational companies are in a position to control both the production of infrastructures and the transmission of programmes. This *de facto* monopoly is opposed to the establishment of a new international economic order.

The international community should attach as much importance to the balance and diversity of the flows of information as to an attentive examination of the content of that information. In this connexion international agreements should be drawn up on postal communications and telecommunications charges and tariffs; copyright and artistic property; the flow of information and data from one country to another; the international distribution of wavelengths and the use of communication satellites; and data storage and automatic retrieval systems.

The international community should also endeavour to restructure the international telecommunications system, that is to say, make changes in the world communication network map and establish 'communication centres', etc., so that the regions where the developing countries are grouped shall no longer be at a disadvantage. It need hardly be pointed out that communication systems are generally planned along a north-south axis with the result that, to take an example, two adjacent African countries are obliged to pass through European capitals in order to establish communications with each other. This very vast undertaking, which began with the launching of communication satellites, calls for considerable resources, but the infrastructure whose creation it will make possible is absolutely necessary for the establishment of a new economic order.

The international community should, further, consider the elaboration of national information and communication policies as a sphere in which the needs expressed by developing countries should receive priority attention. For technical and institutional reasons, any national information policy must also be conceived in terms of the regional and world environment.

Unesco has already undertaken a series of activities in the field of information and communication. By way of example, mention may be made of the implementation, from 1973 onwards after a very active preparatory period, of a world scientific and technical information programme (UNISIST) which, in close co-operation with similar activities undertaken by other United Nations Agencies, aims to further the transfer of scientific and technical information, particularly by improving the tools of systems interconnexion and by encouraging the training of specialists, the elaboration of policies and the establishment of national networks. Stress is laid on assistance to developing countries, particularly with regard to training and education, and the programme's long-term objective is to establish a flexible network of information services based on voluntary co-operation.

In allied spheres, Unesco provides assistance to its Member States for the development of national documentation, libraries and archives infrastructures under the NATIS (National Information System) programme and it is planned to set up a science and technology policies information exchange system (SPINES) in the near future.

In co-operation with the United Nations Development Programme and other institutions, Unesco has embarked on a number of projects for the development of a rural and local press specially designed for illiterates. It has carried out programmes to encourage the publication of scientific and technical periodicals and of children's magazines.

At its eighteenth session, the General Conference of Unesco stressed the effects on the press and on textbooks of the steep rise in the price of paper and launched an appeal to the developed countries to collaborate 'in making supplies [of paper] and money available to ... the developing countries suffering from the present crisis' (18C/Resolution 4.142).

A message broadcast by radio or television reaches a much wider audience than does any written message. Sixty developing countries, however, have less than 100 radio receivers per 1,000 inhabitants, and 30 or so countries in Asia and Africa have no television transmitters. Elsewhere, the cost of programmes and pressure of public opinion are forcing those in charge to broadcast foreign programmes which have no connexion with local life and are of a low educational value. Unesco's research on the use of radio and television for educational purposes and for development has nevertheless enabled a mass of knowledge to be gathered, on which Member States can draw. Similarly, studies made on the setting up of international communication systems via satellite and microwaves show that it is possible to establish regional systems in Asia and Africa, the Arab States and South America.

It is important that countries should not depend exclusively on international film producers, particularly where educational films are concerned, and that they should seek films better adapted to situations, localities and attitudes. Unesco can make its experience in this respect available to Member States which have no film industry. It can also participate in preparing an international directory of educational and cultural films so as to broaden the range of productions fitted to meet national needs, or capable of being adapted in the light of those needs.

In face of a superabundance of information—the flood of pictures, words and sounds poured out by television, radio and the press—the public has scarcely any way of reacting, expressing its preferences and initiating a dialogue; it remains passive, traumatized or manipulated, and this is unhealthy. Unesco is making studies and holding consultations with professional institutions and is organizing intergovernmental conferences with a view to the elaboration of communication policies, particularly within the Organization's fields of competence—which are education, science and culture—and also to the formulation of international principles for the preparation of national codes of ethics for use by the mass media. Among the questions being dealt with are the accurate and balanced presentation of news and opinions, the presentation of information concerning violence, crimes and sex, the right of reply and the rectification of errors and, lastly, respect for private life.

It should further be recalled that, at its seventeenth session, the General Conference of Unesco adopted the Declaration of Guiding Principles on the Use of Satellite Broadcasting for the Free Flow of Information, the Spread of Education and Greater Cultural Exchange. This Declaration states that: 'Satellite broadcasting shall respect the sovereignty and equality of all States . . . [It] shall be apolitical and shall be conducted with due regard for the rights of individual persons and non-governmental entities as recognized by States and international law' (17C/Resolution 4.111).

For the development of mass communication systems which meet the needs and aspirations and which respect the rights of individuals, societies and the international community, it is necessary to formulate coherent policies and national plans. This is one of the matters in which international co-operation, the basis of a new international economic order, is indispensable.

Stimulation, through the development of the social sciences, of a cultural self-examination by every society, to help it to derive the greatest advantage from the instruments of change without losing its identity

The establishment of a new international economic order should enable the developing countries to achieve a twofold objective: to arrive more rapidly at an independent and integrated development; and to maintain, strengthen or regain their cultural identity.

While respecting cultural pluralism, international co-operation necessarily brings together economic, social and cultural—even political—models, and values bound up with various types of society. How is this meeting to be envisaged so that it may lead to an international order based on equity and equality, such as will engender peace?

One fact should be noted from the outset: the developed countries are in a position to exert a certain cultural influence because of their standard of living, their types of consumption and the forms of knowledge and information that characterize them. They exert this influence consciously or unconsciously, and they are little inclined to question their own ways of life, in which they see a form of modernity that is desirable both for themselves and for others.

The developing countries feel this power as a danger and even as an aggression: a danger of loosing their cultural identity and of never making good their backwardness in relation to the developed countries if they follow the same lines as the latter; a danger, too, of creating divisions within their own people, some of whom are attracted by these forms of modernity and adapt themselves to those forms or copy them to such an extent that they do not hesitate to leave their own country, while others, more rooted in tradition and slower to change, remain aloof from this transformation. What is at stake is therefore serious.

It is not enough to stress the importance of the cultural dimension of development. We must go further and assert that recognition of cultural identity, linked with the mobilization of society, is an essential factor in independence and national development. Every State should thus attach particular importance to a profound study of its national culture, focusing attention on its individual values. In this way, it will be enabled to protect its authenticity from the risks of uprooting or levelling as well as from the new forms of colonialism, and to participate, with equal right and dignity, in the work of international cultural co-operation. This individualization of cultures according to their own specific nature forms the basis for dialogue in mutual respect and appreciation of other cultures.

It is for this reason that Unesco is endeavouring to help Member States to define and develop national cultural policies, in the same way that, since its foundation, it has considered as one of its essential tasks the promotion of cultural exchanges and mutual appreciation between civilizations.

Unesco does not confine itself to working for the preservation of the cultural heritage, but seeks to contribute to the furtherance of cultural development properly so called and to the enlistment of cultural activities in the service of the transformation of societies. It will then be for the societies themselves to choose the economic order best suited to their aspirations, and the least constraining stages and techniques by which to attain to it.

Science and technology in their many forms are the bearers of new cultural values which have to be adapted to the historic content of traditional civilizations. These civilizations, however, can only continue to exist if they, in turn, arouse themselves to respond to the new needs of society.

In this difficult dual encounter—that of a people with its historic culture now re-expressed and that of an age-old tradition with the modern aspects of science and technology—the contribution of the social sciences and humanities is indispensable, since their functions include exploration and integration.

The task of exploration consists in identifying and studying the essential facts and problems of social and cultural development, with a view to providing governments with the means of taking them into account in the preparation of their plans.

The task of integration consists in making sure that there is convergence between social and cultural thinking and the objective analysis of interrelationships and real possibilities. This second category of task includes study of the general context of international co-operation for development (the role of transnational companies, the rights and duties of States), study of the effects of this co-operation on the personality of each country, and elaboration of a general reflection on the major problems of growth and development viewed from the systematic standpoint of interaction between nations and between regions.

The still somewhat unsatisfactory results of international action for development give grounds for thinking that, despite an initial growth of awareness, international institutions have not taken the human element sufficiently into account or, at least, have underestimated the complexity of the social and cultural factors involved, unwisely excluding from the field of operations everything that might hinder a short-term efficacy. What has suffered thereby is long-term efficacy—the real efficacy—and, for this reason, many of the programmes drawn up in the light of emergencies or particular situations will have to be looked at afresh in proper perspective.

The conquest or reconquest of the independence of

every national community, the definition of its interchanges with the outside world and efforts to achieve the harmonious insertion of the various sections of the population in the joint development endeavour, are all steps which imply a wide use of the methods of the social sciences and a mastery of them, within interdisciplinary contexts. From this standpoint, the activities already carried out by Unesco in the sphere of the social sciences lend support to the principles of a new international economic order and contribute to bringing about the conditions for its establishment. To further its activities in this respect, Unesco intends, where the social sciences are concerned:

To contribute more actively to the strengthening of social science institutions and research, particularly in the developing countries, so that the political, economic and social options of those countries may increasingly be based on appropriate knowledge.

To develop and extend planned studies in the applied social sciences concerning the fundamental problems connected with the idea of, and the conditions for, achieving a new international economic order that shall be more just and more fraternal.

To extend, to study thoroughly and to systematize the contribution of the social sciences to the conception, planning, implementation and evaluation of activities carried out by the Organization in the various fields of its competence.

To examine the complex interrelations between peoples, resources, the environment and development.

By contributing in this way to the advancement of the social sciences applied to the problems of our time, Unesco is playing the part of an effective intermediary between the requirements of action and the pursuit of research.

Conclusion

Although all peoples acknowledge the need for economic and social development, we have as yet no clear idea of what it means or should mean from the quantitative and qualitative points of view. Both developed and developing countries are asking themselves fundamental questions about the meaning of development and false interpretations of it. This is a vital matter, on which the future of thousands of millions of people depends, and not a mere subject for speculation.

If the pattern of development empirically evolved by the industrialized countries and the types of consumption that correspond to it cannot be extended to the majority of mankind—and it is questionable whether this is desirable—our understanding of development and the methods we use to achieve it must be changed. What is more, we must find a satisfactory way of co-ordinating integrated development on an international scale and the promotion of endogenous, independent development for every society.

Unesco must contribute to this search and promote a genuine science of development, a science both social and political, applied and practical.

The present inequalities between peoples and the injustice of international relations have made the developing countries exert a critical pressure upon the world. As a result of this pressure, in itself legitimate, those in power may have recourse to authoritarian solutions or even solutions based on force. This would lead to confrontations fraught with consequences for the whole of mankind, since deprived peoples can resist force and even render it inoperative to a considerable extent if they want to, as both ancient and recent history shows. This is why the establishment of a new international economic order is an opportunity to establish peace which we must not let slip. Nations today are prepared to negotiate and co-operate, but, despite this willingness for dialogue, the threat of arms, whether economic, political, ideological or military arms, continues to hang over mankind, whose future will be most precarious unless practical solutions are rapidly found, by means of which peace can be established on firmer foundations.

This is why Unesco, in contributing to reflection about the establishment of a new international economic and social order and its active introduction into the fields of science, technology, culture, education and information, which are within its competence, wishes, in accordance with its purpose and its history, to serve the progress of peoples and the cause of human rights and peace.

Appendix

Report of the Panel
of Counsellors on Major
World Problems and
Unesco's Contribution
to Solving Them

The *Report* on the work of the Panel of Counsellors on Major World Problems and Unesco's Contribution to Solving Them, which held three meetings in the spring of 1975 at Unesco's Headquarters in Paris, will be found below.

The members of the Panel were as follows:

Yoshio Abe, Professor at the University of Tokyo.

Samir Amin, Director, African Institute for Economic Development and Planning.

M. J. Anstee, Deputy Regional Director, Bureau for Latin America, United Nations Development Programme.

Béchir Benyahmed, Director of the magazine *Jeune Afrique*.

Wilbert Chagula, Minister for Economic Affairs and Development Planning, United Republic of Tanzania.

Jean-Marie Domenach, Director of the review *Esprit*.

Marion Donhoff, Chief Editor of the newspaper *Die Zeit*.

Abdul-Razzak Kaddoura, Rector of the University of Damascus.

Alfred Kastler, Member of the Academy of Sciences, Honorary Professor at the University of Paris, Nobel Prize for Physics.

M. G. K. Menon, Secretary, Department of Electronics, Government of India.

Yehudi Menuhin, Musician.

Charles Morazé, Director of the Institute of Studies for Social and Economic Development of the University of Paris.

Aurelio Peccei, Chairman of the Club of Rome.

Paul Prebisch, Special representative of the Secretary General, United Nations Emergency Operation.

Radovan Richta, Director of the Institute of Philosophy and Sociology of the Czechoslovak Academy of Sciences.

Joaquin Ruiz-Gimenez, Professor at the University of Madrid.

Abdul Aziz El Sayed, Director-General of the Arab Educational, Cultural and Scientific Organization.

Vadim Sobakine, Professor of International Law, Moscow.

As is indicated in Paragraph 1 of the Report, *the text was established by the Secretariat on the basis of a document approved in provisional form, at the end of the third session of the Panel and taking into consideration the drafting changes and suggestions made subsequently by certain participants. It must therefore be born in mind that this text, though setting out in as accurate a manner as possible the ideas of the Panel, does not necessarily express, on all points, the unanimous opinions of its members.*

Introduction

1. The Panel of Counsellors set up by the Director-General to analyse major world problems and advise on the contribution which Unesco might make to solving them, held three sessions in Paris at the Headquarters of the Organization from 22 to 24 April, from 27 to 29 May, and from 25 to 27 June, 1975. This report was adopted, in provisional form, at the close of the third session, on the understanding that members of the Panel could, within a period of six weeks, present suggestions for specific amendments to the text of the report and comments to be published as an Annex.[1] The final text was established by the Secretariat, on the basis of the answers received. In a number of cases it seemed necessary to mention in footnotes, disagreements expressed by certain members of the Panel or suggested redrafting of various sentences in so far as they differ significantly from this text.

2. The meeting was opened by the Director-General, who emphasized the importance attached to the work of the Panel, notably with a view to establishing closer ties between Unesco and international scientific, intellectual and artistic circles. It is the Organization's duty, within the United Nations, to encourage serious thinking about the major problems of concern to mankind

---

1. These comments are not reproduced in this edition of the report.

at the present time, and to provide guidance for the international community as a whole. It must also establish its future programmes on revised bases. Intellectual co-operation, far from being in opposition to action designed to promote development, is closely linked with it, development constituting the essential element of the world's problems as a whole. The Director-General indicated the working methods, more especially in relation to the medium-term plan of the Organization.

3. During its second session, the Panel of Counsellors held a joint meeting with the *Ad Hoc* Working Group on Youth, which assists the Secretariat in developing Unesco's Youth Programme. The exchanges of views at this meeting dealt in particular with the attitude of young people to Unesco.

I   Extent and significance of the present crisis

4. The first and main concern of the Panel was the present threat to mankind as a species. We are now undergoing a period of profound and rapid, though uneven, and not infrequently crisis-ridden change. This change is largely connected with the ever-increasing power available to man, through the development of science and technology. The roots of the crisis phenomena lie, however, in the crucial sphere of social relations, which to a considerable degree are still not sufficiently adapted to cope with the rapidity of change caused by science and technology. Technology is ambivalent. On the one hand, it has brought immense benefits to mankind. On the other, it has resulted in an incredible accumulation of destructive devices. Furthermore, the contradictions in the transfer of technology from the industrial centres to the developing areas of the world, with their characteristic socio-economic structures, have brought very serious maladjustments and disruptions. Inequalities have been accentuated and an extraordinary demographic growth is taking place. Millions of young people are being led to doubt and protest, and soon perhaps to despair with its accompaniment of violence.[1]

1. Deletion of this sentence was recommended by several members of the Panel. A majority, however, favoured its retention.

5. One thing is beyond doubt: none of the urgent problems facing mankind today and tomorrow can be solved successfully if the conditions of peace are not ensured if the relaxation of international tension is not transformed into an irreversible process and if the enormous resources, today still tied up with armaments, are not gradually released for human development. Efforts for the consolidation of peace, which is to be understood as a just and democratic system of international relations based on the principles of peaceful coexistence and not simply as absence of war, should be expanded in all spheres, ranging from economics to science, from diplomacy to culture. Each step forward in any of these directions (including science, culture and education) can prove decisive. Existing stocks of nuclear weapons are already capable of liquidating several times the population of the world. Furthermore, several hydrogen bombs are manufactured each day, a hundred times more powerful than the Hiroshima bomb. Annual expenditure on the armaments race is very probably around 200 to 250 billions of dollars—a sum equal to the total national income of countries in which the majority of mankind is living. At the same time, twenty-five hundred million men and women largely live a precarious existence at levels of nutrition well below the acceptable minimum. The present growth rate of these populations is such that their number is expected to double in twenty-five years. It is mainly the release of means still devoted to armaments that could provide the material basis conducive to settlement of the problems of development in the world of today.[1]

6. The currently accessible resources of the earth have their limits. Within the space of a few generations we are fittering away reserves of energy below the ground which nature has taken thousands of millions of years to accumulate. As for solar energy, which

1. Deletion of this sentence was suggested by several members of the Panel, who felt that the problem of development cannot be reduced to that of the transfer of financial resources. Mr Richta suggested it be replaced by the following text: 'Each advance towards international détente and the consolidation of peaceful co-operation releases immense resources essential for the solution of all other major world problems. At the same time, it paves the way towards further advances in the same direction.' Miss Anstee suggested the text: 'A marked reduction in the resources that are today devoted to armaments could make a significant material contribution towards the solution of the world's development problems.'

could possibly solve this problem, it calls for the development of highly advanced technologies. In the immediate future there is a danger that we shall destroy, without a thought for future generations, the plants and trees produced over the ages by photosynthesis. In fifty years, nine-tenths of the forests of some tropical islands have disappeared; many forests are being ravaged by the paper industry, on which the press of several industrialized countries, as well as certain industries and commercial interests, in particular for packaging purposes, make excessive demands. The equatorial forest is being attacked in turn. The future is also being jeopardized through excessively primitive exploitation of natural resources by famished groups of human beings whose pressing needs are destroying resources which, if exploited rationally, would help to ensure future progress.

7. Under the pressure of justified or artificial imperatives to maintain growth, to increase consumption or satisfy it heedlessly, today's generations, already much more numerous than their predecessors, are plundering and polluting nature in a somewhat irresponsible manner and condemning future generations, which will be even more numerous, to live in seriously degraded environments.

8. Thus, the very fact that resources, whether renewable or not, are limited, shows that the 'Western model of development' is not generally applicable either in space or in time. Progress based on this model, until now considered in certain quarters as being potentially capable of extension all over the world, is henceforth faced with fundamental contradictions.

9. In some societies where they are most firmly established, industrialization and technology deprive individuals and groups of the possibility of influencing their living conditions, and hence their own fate. The issue at stake is man's ability to establish a comprehensible and creative relationship between himself, his group and the environment. The rights and freedoms of man are threatened by multiple intrusions into his private life, which, as a result of the spread of computer science and communication techniques, is being conditioned on the basis of surveys which sometimes are more or less purposely inquisitorial. Thus some of the industrialized countries must undertake a new kind of struggle to defend the rights of man, the very notion of which is an empty promise for the masses of the developing countries who are deprived of the most elementary means of satisfying their needs.

10. These considerations emphasize the close interdependence of the problems facing the modern world. The over-all nature of the approach required to solve them must be recognized; we are not faced with distinct problems, each of which we may try to solve separately and in isolation. We are dealing with a complex whole in which mechanisms or phenomena are closely interrelated, acting or reacting on one another. The world must be considered as a totality or a system, whose parts are organically linked. It is essential to consider the whole network of problems, in its interrelatedness and inner structure.

11. A global view must therefore be a prerequisite to any attempt to solve the different problems of today. The United Nations declaration on a 'New International Economic Order' can be regarded as an event of world-wide significance attesting to the joint endeavours of nations to achieve a positive settlement of urgent problems of present-day socio-economic development. The introduction of a 'New International Economic Order' obviously concerns not only economics, but is also a matter of social, scientific-technological and cultural relevance, and one that presents a great challenge to scholarship in all branches of social sciences throughout the world.

12. The problems of peace, of the rights of man, and of the survival of mankind are not to be separated from the problems of development itself. For this reason we should look beyond economic development. What is necessary is to seek an optimal and global socio-economic solution which will benefit all mankind. We must therefore give up thinking of the centres of economic power as the sole repositories of truth, civilization and universality.

13. It has been held in certain quarters that industrial growth, along the lines of certain European or North American centres, would itself bring about a general improvement in human conditions, each nation being free to reproduce the proposed pattern for itself. We must face the fact that this is not so.

14. The development process of the industrial centres was innovatory, but the kind which takes root in the developing countries is mainly imitative, and lacks social, technological or ideological authenticity as well as originality in institutions or patterns of consumption. Unable to bring about social integration or to correct disparities, capitalism in developing countries accentuates existing contradictions. Importation of productive techniques

requires a continuously increasing ratio of capital per person employed; it tends to economize on labour even when labour happens to be the abundant factor. Exogenous industry, indeed, offers far fewer jobs than endogenous industry did in the developed countries at the time when their level of investment was what it is today in the developing countries, but in quite a different context. To avoid unemployment and under-employment in the poorer countries, the rate at which capital is accumulated must be very much greater, but this is made impossible by a pattern of consumption which imitates that of the rich industrial centres and favours solely the privileged sectors of the population, and by the fact that the local accumulation potential leaks away towards such centres. Most of the rural population and a high proportion of those who live in towns are cut off from the growth process. Under these circumstances, there is a pressure either to restrict the consumption of the upper strata of the population, or curb the demands of the lower strata.[1] In both cases, the economic problems require serious choices of a political or social or ethical nature.

15. Once it is seen as global, development can no longer be the direct extension to the whole world of the knowledge, ways of thought, life styles or experiences specific to a single region of the world; each local development must be related to its own values and culture. It is not enough to transfer the sum total of the knowledge available in developed countries to the developing countries; to do this excludes the possibility of any genuine implantation of science and technology in the countries at the receiving end. It favours the 'brain drain' and even slows down the general advancement of knowledge by depriving the creative imagination of access to more varied sources than those on which the existing system drew.

16. It will be noted in the first place that the scientific or technological needs and traditions of the developing countries are such that for purposes of practical application it is necessary to ensure that knowledge and processes are adapted to the special conditions of development and to the specific socio-economic and cultural features of these countries. In addition, there is some

1. A member of the Panel, R. Richta, asked for the deletion of this sentence, stating that 'the alternative involving the curbing of the demands of the lower strata is simply unacceptable'.

evidence of the value of 'home grown' procedures which may lead to the emergence of new scientific and technological knowledge. Furthermore, many fundamental discoveries are neither purely individual nor fortuitous. They are linked with social motivations, and scientists are dependent on their membership of society.

17. Scientists should conduct their research by deriving their motivations and inspiration from their environment. A sort of monopolization of science, aggravated by the 'brain drain', prevents advantage being taken of the diversity of living conditions and cultures capable of stimulating innovations. For instance, with a view to the application of solar energy, certain kinds of fundamental research should perhaps have been carried out in tropical countries, notably in the field of semi-conductors or the conservation of energy, such research having been neglected in temperate or cold countries, especially when supplies of coal and oil seemed to be inexhaustible and cheap.

Photo-synthesis will find a further application in the horticultural or agricultural practices of non-temperate countries. Old-established usages may assume an innovatory significance provided traditional customs are studied and are not the subject of scorn, as they still are among those who hold artificially preconceived ideas on 'modernity'.

18. At all events, the immediate problem facing the developing countries is that of establishing an infrastructure for science. As long as this does not exist, as long as these countries do not possess their own indigenous scientific capability, there can be no authentic scientific development, but only transplantation of imported science, which does not correspond to the true needs of the country, and whose value, expressed in terms of its contribution to over-all scientific progress, is questionable. It is therefore a task of the utmost importance and urgency to establish everywhere the local bases of real scientific development, that is to say, to constitute, maintain and animate an indigenous scientific potential establishing and widening as many contacts as possible with the people around it. As there can be no original indigenous scientific development without an original indigenous civilization and traditions, a prerequisite is to be found in the awareness of such a civilization and its values.

19. If it has been feared that science and technology are escaping from man's control, it is because science has too often

been considered as an independent variable. Actually, science is a product of history and of society, and it owes just as much to the social environment as to the work of the scientists. It is only by taking these mutual interactions into account that we can learn to define new strategies and priorities which are just as valid for social progress as for world scientific progress. Every advance in the natural sciences should then be a accompanied by an analysis of its implications for society. Far from halting or slowing down progress, this procedure, associating the human sciences with the natural sciences, would widen the bases of progress and open up many new perspectives.

20. Whilst science has been concerned with discovering knowledge and understanding nature, its applications have been largely governed by the profit motive to the benefit of small sections of human society—groups or countries; and indeed, in this process, distortions have crept into the priorities for the growth of science itself. We would also like to draw attention to the huge sums spent on scientific research, half of which at least are spent on armaments which become obsolete or cancel one another out as quickly as possible; and to the sums which are spent on stimulating and attempting to satisfy unnecessary needs of the consumer system. An orientation of scientific and technological development, basically lacking any underlying commitment to over-all social progress, has given rise in many quarters to a feeling of 'frustration' and 'disillusionment', to a call for the 'containment of science' and for the 'taming' of technology, ultimately resulting in fear and hatred towards science and technology in general. In actual fact, science is one of the great creative manifestations of human genius. What is needed is a new concept and long-range international strategy for the development of science and technology which reflects over-all global social needs—a concept and strategy that should not and must not, in their rational advance, become detached from the basic human orientation and fundamental values of human life.

21. A concept of science, based on an analysis of the inter-actions between science and society, would result in the formulation of strategies comprising new priorities related to social progress and the solution of the major world problems; it would also encourage the developing countries to work out their own scientific and technical development strategies. Moreover, each step forward

in the natural sciences should be accompanied by a corresponding advance in the social sciences. There can be no question of stopping or slowing down the progress of science; on the contrary, it must be harnessed to the task of solving the most serious problems which confront us.[1]

22. In the current stage of development of science and technology, it is no longer sufficient to seek in isolation mastery over certain natural processes or the development of specific areas. Rather, it is essential to look at the global system as a whole since manipulation of a part of the system, on the current scale, has repercussions at a variety of unexpected points. There is thus need to analyse global problems and to prepare long-range prognoses relating to human needs, world resources, scientific possibilities, etc., on an integrated international basis.

23. We would here draw the attention of Unesco to the fact that, with the headlong progress of science and technology, there are new developments in the offing whose implications are of a global nature for human society as a whole—such as interference with the genetic code, deliberate interference with climate, mass application of omnipresent information systems and storage devices with everlasting memories, industrial utilization of microorganisms, creation of closed man-nature metabolism cycles and so on. Concerning questions of so far-reaching a character, there is need for a widely based discussion leading to a global concept, and in this Unesco should play an important role.

24. A truly sound concept of the future of contemporary civilization can only be based on a parallel development of man and society, on the one hand, and technology on the other. We are entering a period in which — without well thought-out programmes of social development, without a purposeful control of social processes and without a purposeful shaping of the way of life—man's socially useful abilities will be prodigally wasted. We need to realize that the control of social processes is at once the most comprehensive and the most difficult task confronting contemporary science.

---

1. In particular one can mention: the study of the pollution of the oceans and the atmosphere; the study of the advantages and dangers of a massive development of nuclear power stations, producers of energy. (Note by Alfred Kastler.)

25. Culture is not a luxury reserved for those whose elementary needs are satisfied; it is linked with the organization of society, and to it society owes its dynamic force. It is made up of the wisdom of the illiterate or the experience handed down through generations of manual workers as well as of the highest scholarship. Traditions which have been forgotten or destroyed by inconsiderate modernization are irreparable losses to the understanding of our destiny.

26. To over-assert cultural particularities is just as dangerous as to underrate them. It is another way of running the same risks. The constant equilibrium between sciences and cultures must be matched by an equilibrium in mutual efforts at comprehension, and by incessant adjustments between what different cultures have to learn from one another.

27. The processes of education have clearly to be two-way. No educational body can properly transmit what it knows unless it is sufficiently familiar with those to whom it is addressing itself. And since no-one can know everything, mechanisms of balanced exchanges should be established to offset the inequalities of knowledge. The study and setting up of mechanisms of this kind is a task all the more arduous in that it has not yet been attempted. If it had been possible for such equilibria between the two complementary flows of communication to exist spontaneously, the virtues of peace, freedom, equality, and the rights and duties of man would come just as naturally to him as his physiological functions. For example, it has been established that a foreign language is learned all the more easily at school in proportion as the pupil knows how to use his native language. Even learning of the most difficult kind becomes readily accessible to the extent that the learning process is based on experience that has been properly lived and assimilated.

28. True receptivity is the organic complement of effective creativity. Transfers of technology must take this into account; they will only have a future for those at the giving end if those at the receiving end have positively participated in such transfers. The behaviour patterns necessary in a world thrown off course by a crisis resulting from one-way inequalities imply that just as much importance should be attached to trends rising upwards from below as to those which traditionally flow in the opposite direction.

29. It is not to be taken for granted that men will escape the course of events which has led them to the present dangers; the

survival of the planet is at stake. Urgent steps must be taken to make better use of education and information with a view to the rapid adjustment of sciences and cultures; all groups and all countries could dangerously jeopardize the interests of future generations if they fail to agree on this priority need as soon as possible.

30. Yet while taking these urgent measures, to which we should devote all our available resources, is it not high time to display a certain modesty, a wisdom which at times our ancestors possessed and which could constitute the basis of a new morality? What is at stake, indeed, is not merely the survival of the human race, but the survival of all living things. If man really wants to live in harmony with the natural environment, as he claims he does today, he must show respect not only for human rights but also for the rights of life in its widest sense. In other words, man must fully accept the responsibility incumbent upon him for the fate of all living things which are at his mercy, and no longer consider them as mere 'resources' to be exploited.

31. This positive concern is not meant to cover up the wretchedness that still afflicts a large part of mankind. Rather it combines two attacks of the same kind, against human egoism and against an anthropocentric conception detrimental to man himself. To trigger off a moral awareness of these, especially in those highly industrialized countries whose excessive consumption of 'resources' is speeding the destruction throughout the whole world of everything that represents life (not only flora and fauna, but water and air), we must try to go beyond short-term utilitarian solutions and conceive a fraternity based on an enduring sense of world-wide solidarity.[1]

1. R. Richta expressed his disagreement with the contents of Paragraphs 30 and 31. He felt, on the one hand, that morality cannot be based on a relation with nature, for morality is intrinsically linked with interhuman relations; on the other hand that the formulation could be interpreted as rejecting humanism and should therefore be avoided. He recommended that the second and third sentences of Paragraph 31 be replaced by the following text: 'What seems to be necessary here is, rather, to realize the general conditions conducive today to the implementation of ideas of humanism. From now onwards, man must "handle nature" (and this applies not only to flora and fauna, but also to water and air) not in terms of a short-term utilitarian conception but within the framework of a long-term outlook, fully aware of his responsibility

II   The mission of Unesco

A.   *General*

32. Unesco's primordial concern should be the promotion of social justice, for social injustice, like war, is born in the minds of men. Unesco must therefore use its best endeavours to ensure that the New International Economic Order is also translated into a New International Social or Human Order.

33. The fundamental missions of Unesco are determined by the very nature of world problems in general. Of all the United Nations Specialized Agencies, Unesco has the most wide-ranging vocation; it is the only one in a position to consider contemporary problems in their world-wide context and in the light of their interdependence, since they all come within Unesco's sphere in their relation to science, culture, education and information. Unesco, responsible for everything concerning knowledge, ideas and values, should be a trail-blazer for the United Nations system and the entire international community.

34. In this context, the first task of Unesco should be to stress the global character of these problems. It is not merely a question of promoting the idea of world-wide human solidarity as an ethical goal, but also, and above all, of furnishing an over-all interpretation of the world's problems, elucidating in particular the global nature of development. For there is a vacuum in the knowledge of development as a global process. It is necessary to integrate its various elements: technological, economic, social, political and cultural, in order to understand the dynamics of their interdependence. Unesco, which is in a very favourable position to take advantage of the experience gained by other international or national, intergovernmental or non-governmental institutions and centres in their particular fields, could assist in the synthesis of what may be called the science of development—of a global or integral development. It would contribute to the important task of combining all those

---

for mankind's future, for the future of our planet. A workable point of departure, one that can provide a realistic groundwork for the solution of major problems of the present-day world—a sphere where Unesco can make a substantial contribution—is the fostering of an awareness of solidarity among the different nations, the promotion of mutual understanding and mutual peaceful co-operation.'

different elements into a whole, either by stimulating others in their work or by undertaking its own research when necessary. It should, however, also draw on the results of the intensive research already being undertaken in various institutions throughout the world.

35. As there is still no comprehensive and vigorous international programme devoted to this effort of scientific clarification and understanding of the process of development, it is in this area that the new United Nations University could contribute in a decisive way. The Charter of the University requires it to engage in research in the field of development on a world-wide basis and within the framework of a global approach. The institutional links between Unesco and the University will make it possible, and indeed highly desirable, that their programmes, tending towards a common objective, become interrelated in a mutually enriching way. This collaborative work between Unesco and the United Nations University can find its fullest expression when it draws on all the results available in this field within the United Nations system.

36. Analysis of the world's problems also shows that the action taken by people today affects the life of future generations; not only their living conditions but in some cases their survival. Although our societies provide for representation of the living and, even, for example through education and religion, of the dead, no provision is made for the representation of future generations. No arrangements are made to ensure that their basic interests are taken into account. Unesco should consider itself responsible for looking after the interests of the generations of the future. It should carry out or sponsor forward-looking surveys to determine the extent to which the consumer-oriented strata of society today are jeopardizing the chances of mankind tomorrow and the changes required in the social order, both at national and international levels, to remedy this situation. It should also consider ways in which unborn generations could be duly represented when decisions are made which affect their lives.

37. Man is the protagonist in every task in a world which will have a population of some six thousand million by the end of the century. The development of the human being and of his creativity through the promotion of different forms of culture, acceptable to all would make the Organization the privileged forum for a permanent cultural dialogue.

38. The Panel of Counsellors, aware of the interdependence and unity of the problems which it is discussing, is of the opinion that these topics should not be envisaged as chapter headings or objectives on which Unesco's programmes of action would be based, but as general guidelines which could nevertheless give rise to specific initiatives and activities, such as those suggested above. These guidelines will be reflected in the various proposals which emerge from the Panel's discussions and which are presented in terms of the Organization's permanent objectives and different spheres of activity.

39. Unesco must strive for intellectual and moral integrity. This requires a strong sense of commitment on the part of its servants and means that the Organization must remain aloof from national rivalries and not succumb to political or commercial pressures.

40. Unesco should avoid the temptation, arising from the very spread and magnitude of world problems, to fragment its limited resources among a multiplicity of projects and programmes; it should rather concentrate its efforts on a few carefully selected key areas, with a view to achieving a real impact, acting as catalyst, pathfinder and the giver of examples.

B. *Specific Recommendations*

(a) *Human rights*[1]

41. The question of human rights is primarily the responsibility of the United Nations itself. In 1966 the General Assembly adopted

1. Some members of the group stressed that the inequitable international order which has characterized the past quarter of a century has today attained the proportions of a crisis under the growing pressure of the peoples of the Third World who have been its principal victims. This profoundly critical situation of all the national and international aspects of social life throughout the world threatens more than ever before the relative peace which has prevailed during this past quarter of a century, just as it carries increased risks of authoritarian solutions which disregard the rights of man and the rights of peoples and nations. These major concerns must direct the lines of action of all international institutions, including obviously those of Unesco. Yet the responsibility for the defence of human rights and of peace is not incumbent specifically on Unesco or any other institution; it is the responsibility of all national and international social forces, whether institutional or not. This defence calls for much more than 'resolutions' of a general nature

the International Covenant on Economic, Social and Cultural Rights and the International Covenant on Civil and Political Rights. It is to be regretted that, nine years later, because the requisite number of ratifications by Member States has not yet been reached, these Covenants have still not come into force. During the next few years, Unesco should strive, particularly through its education programmes, to promote an awareness of the need to overcome the obstacles—social, economic or political, or deriving from racial or sexual discrimination—which stand in the way of the ratification of these Covenants.[1]

42. It would also be well to consider possible means of devising and adopting more practical measures. These might provide, in a form yet to be determined, for the guaranteeing by the international community of the right of every individual to a minimum standard of living as regards food, housing, medical care and education. It was suggested that, if such rights were effectively guaranteed to everyone, society might, in return, expect the observance of certain obligations.

43. The ideas of responsibility, obligation, and duty, which are inseparable from the idea of rights, may lead to the conclusion that it is particularly important not only to set certain minimum standards, but also and above all certain maxima (e.g. in terms of consumption or income).[2] The study of these limits is related to that of inequalities between nations and individuals and Unesco should promote such studies. Due attention should also be given to the problems of social justice in the fields of education and medical care.

44. The application of rights is the responsibility of each State, and national sovereignty can serve as a protection against

and 'studies' of necessarily limited scope. For this reason these members of the Panel considered that it was not desirable to submit specific recommendations to Unesco on these two fundamental points. It is by giving Unesco new and firmer impetus in the right direction in its own spheres—science, technology, culture and education—that the Organization will be enabled to serve the cause of human rights and peace most effectively. (Note written by Yoshio Abe and Samir Amin.)

1. Since this text was written the number of ratifications has increased substantially thus enabling the two Covenants to come into effect during the first quarter of 1976.
2. Mr Richta mentioned that the stipulation of certain maxima 'can only be feasible for a specific time interval'.

pressures imposing life styles and patterns of thought foreign to communities in which they become the negation of essential rights. It has been said that, in some cases, nationalism is the only asset of countries which do not enjoy sufficient independence or development; but such polarizations are prejudicial, especially if they favour obscurantism and arbitrary power. The principle of national sovereignty does not sanction infringement of certain principles of general validity.

For example, though the laws of ownership may vary, there exist certain fundamental rights of the human condition itself: in particular the freedom of conscience or expression, the right to legal decisions pronounced after public hearings and without torture. Respect of these rights ties in with minimum guarantees and maximum regulations designed to ensure a world order founded on justice.

(b) *Peace*

45. The question of Unesco's contribution to peace was one of the Panel's major concerns. The responsibility for the defence of peace rests with all the institutions in the United Nations system and with all national and international organizations and social forces all over the world. Unesco is not responsible for political measures designed to ensure peace; accordingly, the Panel singled out several proposals which could represent a special contribution by Unesco in its own field of competence to efforts for the consolidation of peace.

46. Unesco should, in the first place, carry out or promote studies and research on the problem of peace, not as the mere absence of war or violence but as a positive state of affairs.

47. The vocabulary of international relations includes terms like 'peaceful coexistence' and 'détente'. Unesco should undertake research with a view to clarifying these conceptions and ways and means of achieving their realization.

48. Unesco should promote studies on ways of reconverting the armaments industry into peaceful activities, giving special attention to the manner in which this might be achieved under various social and economic systems, with minimal detriment to the workers and scientists now engaged in this industry. Such research, together with other measures, would undoubtedly encourage the creation of a psychological climate favourable for

disarmament. Special concern should be given to the possibility of forbidding or at least reducing the arms trade.

49. Unesco should strive by all available means to ensure that science and technology are directed towards human welfare and the betterment of human life. At the same time it is essential to take steps to ensure the conclusion of a convention which would prevent or prohibit military utilization of scientific achievements before these achievements attain operational importance.

50. If peace is to be preserved, violence must be properly understood. The importance of this task requires that encouragement be given to all types of research into the multiple causes of violence—cultural, economic, social, as well as psychological. The results and conclusions of such research should be widely disseminated.

(c) *Science and technology*

51. The analysis which the Panel of Counsellors made of the problems of science and technology brings out clearly the importance of the role that Unesco should play in that sector on a world-wide scale and within the United Nations system. It is Unesco's responsibility to turn its attention to these problems in an over-all context, in relation to all the dimensions of man and the various factors affecting the development of societies, paying special heed to the different forms of cultures and to the future trend of events.

52. Unesco's efforts should bear especially on the relationship between science and technology, on the one hand, and culture and education, on the other. Indeed, it should be noted that the Advisory Committee on the Application of Science and Technology to Development (ACAST) is mainly concerned with the relations between science and the specific ways in which it can be used to promote development. It is this question, for example, that is highlighted in the World Plan of Action prepared a few years ago by ACAST. Unesco should set up an advisory committee similar to ACAST but whose task would be to consider science and technology in a cultural context and in relation to education. Unesco must, of course, be concerned not only with the applications, but also with the development of science.

53. Another major line of emphasis for Unesco might be to promote scientific work in the developing countries, work that would be genuinely rooted in those countries' physical and

human environment, and that consequently would not represent the transplanting of foreign undertakings, nor the transfer or mere continuation of research begun elsewhere. Indigenous scientific communities should be encouraged through appropriate education and training; they should be helped to identify fields that are relatively neglected in the major scientific centres of the industrialized world, the exploration of which might turn out to be particularly fruitful for the developing countries concerned.

54. Unesco might also establish a new type of fellowship enabling scientists from developed countries to work in developing countries, not as experts responsible for the transfer of know-how or the training of 'counterparts', but as actual members of a scientific community engaged in a work programme which that community had itself established and for which it was responsible.

55. These various activities should enable the Organization to help elucidate the relationship between science and different forms of culture and to gain a better understanding of the adaptation of technologies to the environment.

56. It seems essential for Unesco, on the basis of an analysis of the phenomena currently pointing to a crisis in the field of science and technology, to endeavour to work out an international long-term strategy for the development of science and technology, by considering this development in relation to prospects for social progress and change in patterns of living. Thus, Unesco's programme should accord a major place to forward-looking studies with regard to science, technology and society. An approach of this kind presupposes an appreciable contribution from the social sciences and one of Unesco's concerns should be to promote their development so that they may keep pace with the natural sciences.

57. In drawing up and implementing its programme, Unesco should maintain and intensify its contacts and collaboration with the international scientific community, and particularly the scientific unions that make up ICSU. Unesco should also prepare itself to play a key role in the international conference on science and technology which the United Nations is to organize in 1979, conceived in the wider context just described.

58. Lastly, there are services which Unesco would render and which would considerably benefit all countries, whether developing or developed, as well as the whole United Nations system. These services consist in developing an international system of infor-

mation on all branches of science and technology. An important achievement, in this connexion, is the development of the UNISIST international programme. Such a system should facilitate the access of developing countries to data on diversified technologies, and not merely acquaint them with the latest technological and scientific discoveries. This system could also group information on traditional indigenous techniques, and techniques created in the developing countries. It would be worth while devoting a considerable part of the Organization's resources to the development of such a system and to the training of the necessary personnel to put it to efficient use.

(d) *Education*

59. Education is one of the rights whose attainment in practice forms part of all efforts to ensure, by international action, a minimum standard of living for everyone. The need to succeed in eliminating illiteracy once and for all was strongly emphasized. Furthermore, education can and should be instrumental in promoting human rights and creating attitudes favourable to the building of peace. Its function is decisive as regards cultures and the establishment of new scientific communities. It was stressed in particular that Unesco should promote the development of courses on contemporary problems of the world in school programmes, and that such courses should be properly related to past history and the perception of the future.

60. A paradoxical aspect of the subject is that education, recognized as one of the prime means of attaining these objectives, is nowadays being strongly criticized and called into question.

61. A negative assessment has been made of Unesco's educational projects which have furthered the transfer, sometimes without adaptation, of social and economic models specific to the developed countries.

62. In order to enable Unesco to review the main thrust of its activities in the field of education—and this is in accordance with the current policy of the Organization—it must be given the opportunity to try new experiments. Initiatives of this kind call for adequate resources and the acceptance of a number of risks. Naturally, Unesco cannot carry out such experiments alone; it must co-operate with various regional or national institutions. It can, however, play a decisive role as a catalyst.

63. The essential aim of such innovative experiments should be to stimulate educational activities that will make it possible to develop creativity, instead of being concerned simply with the transfer of know-how. Hitherto, education in the developing countries has largely consisted in passing on skills, particularly scientific and technical ones, worked out elsewhere in response to other problems. The material and intellectual resources at Unesco's disposal must be used not so much to support 'conventional' forms of education as to promote experiments that tend to develop creativity, as well as innovation.

64. It was suggested that Unesco should work to develop a conception of education as 'the development of human resources'.

65. Two of the main hopes pinned on education—the improvement of social opportunity and of work prospects—have been greatly frustrated in the last decades. This has affected a certain number of countries, both developing and developed. In fact, the very significant increase in the provision of education, spurred in the first place by a concern for giving a chance to the least advantaged children, has too often led to the exact opposite of its aim. Many of these children find themselves severely discriminated against by the selection procedure imposed by higher education institutions as a result of the increasing numbers of applicants. A similar paradox has occurred in the field of employment. The exclusive gearing of education to university entrance has led to a situation whereby those of the students who cannot secure admission find themselves without the alternative of a vocational training that could prepare them for a productive life. Unemployment with the concomitant features of frustration and violence are often their only lot. It must, however, be admitted that if educational services were distributed on a more equitable basis a correspondingly greater number of suitable jobs would have to be made available, and this would in the main only be possible in the context of a very different pattern of economic development.

(e) *Culture*

66. The relationships between the trend towards a world-wide culture and the individual cultures constitute a major world problem at the present time. It is with this in view that studies should be undertaken to clarify the relationships (and possible

conflicts) between culture and efforts to circulate information and knowledge.

67. Unesco should encourage the initiatives and efforts of each cultural group to obtain a better knowledge of the constituent elements of its own culture, not with the sole aim of preserving these elements and enhancing their scientific and moral value, but in order to help each cultural group realize its cultural identity to the full and establish itself as an entity (and not as a subject of investigation from without). This is the essential prior condition to a genuine world-wide interaction between cultures.

68. Additional efforts should be made to help fit particular cultures into a more diversified and unified conception of world development. While specific features should be encouraged, care should also be taken to prevent their accentuating the danger of confrontations. It is recommended that the teaching of local customs, languages, religions and laws be placed in a world perspective, in the field of aesthetics, local elements should be reassessed, while at the same time knowledge of exogenous forms of expression should be promoted. In the field of information, Unesco should make available documentation on achievements relating to the enriching of the common patrimony, and subjects for discussion designed to contribute to the solution of conflicting situations.

69. The activities of Unesco in the cultural sphere should be one of the essential bases for the attempt at synthesis to which reference was made in Paragraph 34 above, and whose purpose would be to achieve a truly global interpretation of development.

(f) *Information*

70. Unesco's vocation in the field of information must be asserted; the importance attached by the General Conference to the subject 'communication between persons and exchange of information'—one of the four 'problem areas' which Unesco's programme should cover—is quite justified.

71. Unesco should step up its own activity where the information of the public is concerned, not so much to make itself known to world opinion as to communicate certain messages of a fundamental nature. Unesco should have radio and television time made available to it in all Member States, so that it can make known the discussions which are held under its auspices and the results achieved. In this manner, the Organization would help to

make public opinion aware of the great problems which have a bearing on the survival of mankind.[1]

72. It would also be appropriate for Unesco to encourage users' extended participation in the field of audio-visual media, in the form of experiments made with closed-circuit or cable television as well as local programmes. Radio and television stations should not be a hindrance to such initiatives. The ensuing experience could provide a subject for special inquiries and recommendations which would outline the prospects for mass media in the development of culture.

73. The essence of this task is to persuade world opinion that problems are global, that the world in all its diversity is a universe of interdependent factors, that there exists a fundamental solidarity between human beings, and that solutions based on conciliation serve the interests of everyone.

(g) *European co-operation*

74. Whatever the priority given to the problems faced by the developing countries, the role of Unesco is world-wide. Every country and every region deserves Unesco's attention. It must, for instance, be remembered that Unesco is the only organization dealing with science, education, culture and information which includes both Eastern and Western European countries among its members.

It therefore has an indispensable role to play in pan-European co-operation. Amongst the subjects taken up by the Conference on European Security and Co-operation, at present in its final phase, the third 'basket' of problems concerns Unesco. The Organization will have to play a full role in implementing the decisions of this Conference in due course.

---

1. Mr Richta suggested the following reformulation: 'Unesco should regularly make accessible to individual countries and their respective responsible institutions radio and television programmes that would regularly be incorporated into the transmission schedules of these countries in accordance with their specific established rules and regulations. In this way, Unesco could ensure a higher degree of well-informedness of the public with regard to programmes and discussions held under its auspices as well as about the results achieved.'

III Unesco's programme: procedures, ways and means

75. As the Director-General pointed out, Unesco has passed through two phases since its foundation: a phase of international co-operation mainly of an intellectual nature, followed by another phase in which operational activities have acquired considerable importance. In this connexion, the Panel of Counsellors wishes to pay tribute to the efforts deployed and the work carried out in both these areas.

76. It was and still is Unesco's duty to observe, study and make known all the transformations affecting the activities of mankind in its sphere of competence. It must set an example where necessary adaptations have to be made, and help as best it can all those who work in this direction. It may be wondered, however, whether the increasing burden of operational activities, as at present conceived, has not worked to the detriment of this essential function.

77. It must be recognized that at a time when rapid changes are taking place as at present, planning for an extended future should avoid excessive rigidity in programmes and commitments. Though one is bound to commend the intentions laid down in the relevant documents, notably the most recent—'Analysis of Problems and Table of Objectives' (18C/4)—it may be questioned whether the extreme fragmentation of projects, each of them endowed with meagre resources, meets the real needs of flexible planning. One gains the impression that while considerable attention has been given to activities inevitably of a permanent or semi-permanent nature, an insufficient effort has been made to reflect upon some of the key problems that block progress in the present conjuncture of events, to mobilize the resources needed to clarify them, and to make known, as a matter or urgency, information and views designed to lead to effective action.

78. The General Conference decides upon the activities and the budget of the Organization in accordance with a draft which has to be prepared in advance with the aim of satisfying as large a majority as possible. This being so, the margin of initiative left to each delegate and the repercussions which may be expected from the most innovative statements are extremely limited. The decisions as a whole admittedly conform to criteria of prudence that would

be reassuring if the situation were static, but which are not the most effective in response to unforeseen or rapidly changing circumstances. It seems that the budget discussion as a whole is governed by a prior decision concerning the total amount of revenue, in which case any new commitment depends on the cancellation of projects in progress, and this, as everyone knows, is technically and politically difficult.[1]

79. It is therefore not surprising that in many countries Unesco has not acquired the place it deserves. Except in certain fortunate cases, the Organization is not well known enough to the public; its work receives little report or comment or sometimes meets with a certain scepticism.

80. The fact that Unesco has not entered sufficiently into national intellectual and cultural life explains the ignorance, indifference or reserve with which the Organization is regarded by the great majority of young people in a number of countries. As for National Commissions, which are statutorily associated with the work of the Organization, they are specially valuable in countries where relationships between the State, science and culture are close, but elsewhere their authority may be doubtful.

81. The group could not adequately study the decision-making processes of Unesco, but has the impression that they do not assure the necessary flexibility to transform an organization, which is becoming more and more self-contained, into a centre of exchanges and activities widely open to scientific and intellectual communities.

82. It has, however, made an attempt to suggest answers to such questions as: Why is Unesco not more firmly rooted in world intellectual activities? Why are its activities so often unknown? Why have its efforts been so inadequately rewarded? These questions arose during the discussions of the Panel of Counsellors, and some proposals were made under five headings: improving communication, promoting discussions on major issues, making use of the best experience available, stimulating the sharing of knowledge, increasing flexibility.

1. Miss Anstee felt that she could not agree with the implication of this sentence, as any budget discussion must be predicated on some concept of the total resources available, since the latter can never be unlimited.

(a) *Improving communication*

83. Unesco has acquired a language of its own. The special nature of this language often disconcerts those who do not have long experience of working with the Organization; it restricts genuine understanding of the ultimate aims of the Organization's programmes to small groups of initiates; it discourages those delegates who, though they are real specialists, lack familiarity with the procedures specific to Unesco.

84. But this relative obscurity does not correspond to either greater richness or greater precision. It is often the result of an attempt to reconcile divergent and sometimes contradictory views by reaching an agreement which may be superficial and purely verbal.

85. It is also a language which might appear disappointing because, while giving an impression of decision and action, it does not change real conditions in the world. It is necessary for Unesco to change its language. This is one of the conditions on which the extension of its audience and its influence depends.

86. The fact of Unesco's role being known or not is, in itself, not a criterion of the Organization's effectiveness, and the utility of an action designed to promote the 'image' of Unesco seems, in itself, open to question. On the other hand, Unesco must seek in public opinion the support necessary for its activities, and this it can only find if it expresses itself in meaningful terms and if it reflects the same concerns as those of public opinion. Consequently, Unesco must at the opportune moment crystallize and express latent trends and provide responses to matters of concern which arise. Because it has not succeeded in deciphering the meaning of developing trends in recent years, Unesco has left to other bodies less representative of the nations of the world as a whole, the privilege of giving expression to the most pressing questions, albeit sometimes in controversial terms, but nevertheless giving rise to large-scale international discussion of contemporary problems.

(b) *Promoting discussions on major issues*

87. However competent and active the body of international civil servants may be, and however carefully composed its teams of experts, Unesco would go counter to the lessons life teaches us if it took account only of unanimous opinion. By shying away from all subjects of disagreement we allow them to worsen of their own

accord. At least part of the funds, maybe a small part initially, should therefore be allocated to a restricted number of very important discussions. The Organization would have neither to express its opinion as to their substance, nor to prejudge the results.

88. Some fundamental discussions should be brought by scientific experts before the public which they concern. These people would not be invited to reach agreement, but to clarify so far as possible their respective positions. One or more aspects of the 'New International Economic Order' could be chosen; the expression at the present time covers different realities, interests and intentions: a clarification is therefore desirable.

89. The intellectual authority of Unesco depends in large part on how the Organization succeeds in associating the international intellectual community with its activity, in obtaining the support and participation of the individuals, organizations and institutions which form this community.

90. But it is essential to avoid an approach which would portray Unesco as a guardian of ideas through which enlightenment is to be brought to the masses. Idealistic intentions and declarations have shown themselves to be ineffective. They easily become moralizing and paternalistic attitudes liable to meet with rejection rather than acceptance. A certain form of idealism also carries the risk of being confused with the defence of a given system of values, a 'model' system with which Unesco identifies itself and presumes to impose on the whole world. A trend in this direction might cause Unesco to lose its true universality, which is based on the recognition of different forms of culture.

(c) *Making use of the best experience available*

91. Unesco has already published a number of brilliant syntheses, for example, the *History of the Scientific and Cultural Development of Mankind,* and reports on the state of the natural sciences and the state of the human sciences. These works have two shortcomings: they are sometimes too general to be of interest to specialists, and they are too voluminous or too technical to attract a sufficiently wide public. Above all, each of them has been produced only once, that is to say, they reflect a stage of advancement which already today is of interest only as a document. Some of these undertakings, moreover, are excessively monolithic and costly.

92. These works should be periodically updated. For example,

views on history held twenty years ago are seldom valid today; moral problems raised by scientific research have been posed in new terms since biology has been the subject of as much concern as high energy physics was formerly. The same is even more true where the human sciences are concerned. But if the objective aimed at is to be achieved under optimum conditions, would it not be advisable to broaden the scope of the procedures, associating the maximum number of institutions with these tasks rather than having recourse merely to a small group of individuals selected by Unesco? The Organization's role would then be one of stimulation and consultation until such time as a major discussion can be opened up in clear terms, or until general agreement among the specialists is reached spontaneously, in which case the fact must be made widely known.

93. The controversies raised by traditional forms of education, or by differences of cultures, or again by important aesthetic trends, are such that investigations of this type deserve to be extended to cover these subjects.

94. Serious thought should be given to the advisability of Unesco's divesting itself of the great burden of 'operational' activities which have come to absorb so much of the Organization's resources and efforts and which too often have meant the handing down ('one-way traffic') of approaches, techniques and 'solutions' that are alien to the needs and values of the society concerned, and harmful rather than beneficial, at any rate in their long-term effects. The accent should be on research and experiment from which general conclusions can be obtained—the 'multiplier effect'—rather than on operational activities directed towards specific and circumscribed ends.

95. This does not mean that Unesco should abandon involvement in scientific and cultural exchange, but that its main concern should be to foster co-operation for development, rather than technical assistance or technical co-operation as understood in the past. The emphasis should be on the exchange of experience, rather than on the transfer of resources (whether financial or technical). This could cost a great deal less in material terms than present 'operational' programmes, but a great deal more in terms of imagination, innovation and intellectual effort generally. Experience can only be acquired by living it. Unesco could perhaps become the vehicle for enabling key people in education, science and culture to 'live' each

others' experience—particularly when innovative approaches are being adopted—and to synthesize those aspects of them that seem capable of universal application. Another feature of this new approach would be that instead of 'operating' directly, Unesco would indirectly stimulate action through 'centres of excellence' carefully selected in all regions of the world. This would not only enhance the 'multiplier effect' but would also enable Unesco to become a 'centre of excellence' itself, by orchestrating the scattered talents of the best scientific, cultural and educational institutions of both the 'centre' and the 'periphery'.

(d) *Stimulating the sharing of knowledge*

96. The rising cost of publications and the competition they have to face poses the problem of whether Unesco can reasonably occupy a place in this field, when there is so much to be done to aid and co-ordinate what already exists and to encourage spontaneous initiatives.

97. If they are of high quality, the contributions produced by Unesco—under its incentive or with its aid—will always find a place in existing publications, where they will be brought to the notice of interested readers. It is only in certain exceptional cases that suitable subsidies should be used to facilitate the publication of contributions judged to be of international importance. Another type of financial intervention that might be envisaged would aim to ensure that the publication of findings which are significant in several fields or for several countries, is not restricted by the exclusive rights of publishers. All the above considerations apply to specialized work for the benefit of which it would be best to use and adapt existing facilities.

98. However, Unesco should not be deprived of any media of expression, provided that they are of the requisite standard and properly managed. This could provide an opportunity for presenting specific subjects and making the Organization's activities known. There is no reason to believe, *a priori*, that such a measure would not be profitable as well as beneficial. In the case of messages that are of essential significance but which do not fit into the framework already described, there should be no hesitation in incurring the costs of circulating them, even if they have to be distributed free of charge.

99. It may be hoped that as a result of a very open policy such

as that just proposed, Unesco will before long find new opportunities opening up so that soon thereafter the only difficulty will be to choose between them. The Organization itself would then have to make the necessary selection, but in doing so it would draw upon the competence acquired through these various kinds of participation.

100. It is one of Unesco's essential missions to promote the introduction of information on different forms of culture and of the concept of an interdependent world community and of peaceful co-operation into teaching and textbooks as well as into all books intended to maintain literacy. In some of the developed countries, deep-rooted intellectual traditions account for the fact that in school textbooks inadequate attention is given to the best achievements and thoughts of other nations. This is doubtless one of the few fields in which Unesco's endeavours are irreplaceable and to which it must therefore devote an appropriate share of its resources.

101. Educational institutes in some European countries had such influence during the period of colonial expansion that in the areas of their previous influence it is still customary to place the highest value on what they teach. This is true in a sufficient number of cases to justify a great many transfers of knowledge from the 'centre' to the 'periphery'. But the international community cannot remain indifferent to instances in which the reverse is the case. Encouraging the widest exchanges of knowledge of the most diverse kinds, and also the efforts of those who attempt to draw from this diversity some valid lessons for everyone, should be an important task for Unesco.

102. This effort would initially be directed at the teaching of history, but also at philosophy and law, but would also be concerned with other disciplines. It should not neglect the ways in which scientific knowledge has been enriched and transmitted as well as the most successful forms of aesthetic expression. Without putting itself too much to the fore and arrogating a monopoly to itself, Unesco should encourage schools throughout the world to prepare future public opinion in this way and thus spread understanding of those problems which threaten mankind.

(e) *Increasing flexibility*

103. Unesco has been criticized for its excessive centralization. A genuine synthesis of intellectual and cultural currents throughout

the world cannot be achieved without a genuine decentralization of activities on the part of Unesco. If Unesco is to reflect the needs, achievements and aspirations of the 'periphery', it must receive, and heed, the authentic voice of the 'periphery'. Hence, there must be a real decentralization of structures, functions and authority. This would not require additional financial or human resources, nor would it involve excessive bureaucratization, provided that the existing resources at the centre are efficiently redeployed and more effective use is made of the existing regional and subregional structures through greater delegation of authority. Indeed, to the extent that Unesco divests itself of its operational functions in their traditional form, as suggested elsewhere in this report, bureaucracy would recede rather than advance, less over-all resources would be required rather than more, and greater impact achieved in return for a smaller outlay.

104. Such decentralization cannot be expected without a new mentality. So long as it is overburdened with tasks imposed by a programme that is infinitely divided up into separate portions, Unesco will not be able to reverse the present trend. Without in any way diminishing responsibility where the General Conference is concerned, the Secretariat should have a margin of initiative enabling it to give consideration to local requirements and initiatives. In this way, top-level deliberations would no longer be concerned with an over-lengthy series of projects, but with general guidelines, which would place it at a much higher level.

105. From the point of view of forms of organization and action, such an orientation demands closer attention to social and cultural realities throughout the world; closer contacts with regional and local bodies which, by definition, are more closely in touch with these realities; a decentralization of certain activities, notably training programmes, which should be implemented in the developing countries to a greater extent than at present; and a more balanced distribution within the Secretariat, it being noted that the criterion of nationality alone is not always sufficient, for often nationals of many countries have, through their training and education, become so identified with European or North American culture that they no longer genuinely reflect the aspirations and feelings of their countries of origin. It is important that decentralization should make its effects felt not only during the implementing of the programme, but at the actual stage of conception

of the programme, so that regional and local outlooks may be taken into consideration.

106. It may be pointed out here that Unesco is far from possessing the resources to implement, on its own, all measures essential to its mission. This can only be accomplished by associating with its work all national or international bodies working along the same lines. Neither would Unesco have to assign strictly defined tasks, covered by too rigid contracts, to the institutions thus associated. Here again, margins of initiative and freedom of action would increase responsibilities and make controls more simple and effective.

107. These reforms in mentality could lead to reforms in structure. For example, in addition to the division into broad disciplines, there would transversely be a distribution of tasks, less permanent and more mobile, related to pluridisciplinary objectives selected in the light of their importance or their urgency.

108. As soon as any problem arises which merits the attention of the international community, and which falls within the orbit of Unesco, the Organization should be able to constitute an adequate team to deal with it, not to find a solution, but to trigger off awareness of the problem, of the interest it deserves, the demands it implies, and the discussions to which it gives rise. Without claiming to solve the problems of war, famine or ignorance, Unesco would expose them to the full, and would examine the best strategy to help those whose task it is to solve them.

109. Under these circumstances, the Organization's budget should be prepared and decided upon with the greatest possible flexibility. Its implementation would be controlled less by a verification of the conformity between the detailed instructions and strict carrying out of those instructions, as by a careful evaluation of the results achieved. The greatest freedom of procedure would have as a counterpart the possibility of putting a prompt end to sterile expenditure.

110. The documentation produced should be as accessible as possible, that is to say, compact, concise, and written in a readable style.

111. Where the effectiveness of Unesco's operations is concerned, we must take care to avoid adopting either of two extreme attitudes. If excessive illusions as to Unesco's possibilities in this respect are nourished, then there is a risk of disappointment,

yet pessimism is equally inappropriate. The role of Unesco is not so much to set itself guidelines for action which, in most cases, is up to Member States themselves. Unesco must be a laboratory for working out ways in which action is to be taken, and its own operations must first and foremost serve as an example. Thus what counts in Unesco's action is research and experimentation to encourage creativity and to train people who wish to undertake, and are capable of undertaking, new tasks. It is in this light that Unesco's work on behalf of Member States ought to be seen; but this can only be so if we abandon the notion that a ready-made solution can be provided. What must be done is to seek new solutions through genuine co-operation, so that through a veritable exchange there emerge ideas and ways and means corresponding to the real demands of each society.

112. With regard to the ways in which the programme is to be implemented, it is suggested that Unesco should conduct periodic surveys rather than establish exhaustive reports once and for all. The number of meetings of experts should be limited, and more recourse should be had to contracts with bodies such as universities, research centres, and non-governmental organizations. Special importance ought to be placed on suggestions and proposals emanating from the developing countries, and to 'inter-ethnic creative interaction'. The Organization should concern itself with putting out a number of high-level periodical publications.

113. On several occasions in the course of their proceedings, the members of the Panel of Counsellors noted the value of the initiative taken by the Director-General in setting up a group of independent personalities for the purpose of engaging in an exchange of views of a general nature. They concluded that the opinions expressed by such a group could very usefully complement Unesco's own institutional machinery for laying down guidelines and developing its programme. They consider that it would be advantageous to have recourse once again to a group of the same kind at some future time.

114. There is no question of giving to such a group a permanent character; this would mean adding another piece to the already heavy machinery of the Organization; furthermore, an institutional body might lose the capability of studying the problems of Unesco with a fresh, independent and innovative outlook. What is suggested to the Director-General is that recourse be had,

at appropriate times and under opportune circumstances, to consultations of the same wide-ranging, free and open nature as the discussions which enabled the present report to be written.

115. The Panel of Counsellors discussed, but without reaching agreement on the question, a proposal by one of its members that, bearing in mind that Unesco was a 'wartime baby', the Organization might wish to explore the possibility of revising its Constitution so that it reflects the preoccupations, problems, and aspirations of humanity today, as opposed to those of the vastly different world of thirty years ago.

3589 X